Stagecoach

The real story of coaching across the land based on the
BBC tv NATIONWIDE
film series

written by John Richards,
chairman of the British Driving Society

Dedicated to H Langdon Dowsett who has done so much to interest the young in the art of driving and coaching.

The author thanks Mr & Mrs Sanders Watney for reading this book before it was printed.

And Mr & Mrs Frank Haydon, Mr Tom Ryder, Mr Bernard Mills, Mr George Mossman, Mr Jack Watmough, Mr Alan Scales, Mr & Mrs Michael Bale and family, Mrs Chris Eyre, Miss Joy Claxton and Mr George Almond.

The chapter on the filming of *Stagecoach* contains some of the original script of the programme which was put at the author's disposal by Martin Young.

Published by Watmoughs Limited and Horse Drawn Carriages Limited by arrangement with the British Broadcasting Corporation and printed by Watmoughs Limited

ISBN 0 903775 04 2

Contents

The Nationwide *Stagecoach* film unit   4

The passenger and the reporter   5

Filming of *Stagecoach*   7

Early history   17

John Palmer   20

The mail coaches   22

The mail guards   27

Chaplin   29

Turnpike trusts   31

Thomas Telford   33

The coach horse   37

Accidents   39

Quicksilver and the Exeter Mail   43

Coaching characters   46

Coaching customs and conduct   48

The Golden Age   51

Change and decay   54

Highway robbery   56

Coaching painters   59

The Coaching revival and James Selby   61

The Americans   69

A most unusual road   73

Four-horse driving clubs   75

Brakes   77

Driving a team   78

Old Lal on the Great North Road   80

The Tantivy Trot   81

On and off the road   82

The masterful mind   94

"Walk on"   96

The Nationwide *Stagecoach* film unit:

Alan Scales	*producer*
Martin Young	*passenger and reporter*
Colin Munn	*cameraman*
Alex Hansen	*assistant cameraman*
Ron McMorran	*sound recordist*
Dave Mason	*lighting electrician*
Mike Schooley	*film editor*
David Stanford	*initial research*
John Gau	*editor of Nationwide*

The passenger and the reporter

Passenger Young

In the crazy nature of filming, I found myself having to write the concluding words of the *Stagecoach* series almost before we had even seen a stagecoach. We wanted to end by comparing the old coach roads with today's road network, so they stood me on a bridge above the M1 and I said "Down there, as they aim themselves like bullets toward their towns and their cities, do they ever wonder whatever happened to the pioneer spirit that first foresaw the possibility of voyaging across country? Do they ever wonder whatever happened to the romance of travel? No, of course they don't. They're wondering whether they can make Birmingham by twelve-thirty."

And that, I realised there and then, is what our filming was all about—a time when travel *was* an adventure, when to speed with the mails from London to York in just twenty hours was a miracle every bit as significant as today's Concorde miracle, carrying us 3 000 miles in just over three hours.

Coaches, after all, were the first network to run fully "nationwide", and we felt we could amuse and inform our audience with tales of those days—romantic, yes, but tough beyond our modern comprehension.

"My, those coachmen were *hard* men, right boozey old *hard* men" as Tom Parker, himself an octogenarian coachman, had said to me.

So how were we to capture the mood and the look of that age? Well, first find your coach. We found several of the original mail coaches. Secondly, find your background. We asked the police to stop the traffic in the old coaching towns we would visit. And we found out why Britain has so many beautiful old inns: they were built for the coaches, and many are almost unchanged. Thirdly, find yourself a passenger, someone who'll travel the great and direct roads of the land, experience the delights and the discomforts, drink the ale, damn the coachman and submit to the inevitable highwayman. So Passenger Young was born.

He grew up and filled out during the weeks of filming—a moneyed young gent, travelling in the posh inside seats, a bit of a snob, but genuine enough in his love of coach travel, and eager to write his "modest history" of the coach roads of 1830. And Passenger Young's enthusiasm for coaching grew so much that by the time he was forced to travel by rail in the final film, *I* could feel, inside my frock coat and stock, a real fear of the ugly, steaming locomotive that rumbled into the station. This was progress, just like the M3 was to be a hundred years later. It's never so appealing as antiquity.

Passenger Young was clearly going to steal the show, sporting a pink beaver, a green velvet frock coat, waistcoat and half-hunter, and delivering himself of rather grand aphorisms as he trundled to and fro. So what of our menial, the pedestrian old Nationwide reporter? Well, *Reporter* Young clearly couldn't be a pedestrian; he'd never keep up those ten-mile-an-hour averages the coaches could do, so he became a cyclist on a distinctly anti-heroic folding bicycle, which, just for the record, had the most uncomfortable saddle and the lowest gears I've ever encountered. I retired to bed most nights with a sore rear end, and my little legs still going like catherine wheels.

So Passenger Young should travel in style in 1830. Reporter Young should follow him as best he could. And occasionally the two should almost meet. We spent many long, complicated hours trying to give the impression that the two Youngs had just passed by each other in the same frames of the film. But poor old Reporter Young was never allowed to step aboard the old coaches. Only when they stood neglected in a courtyard, their horses gone, their poles drooping, did he get a look in. And there was an embarrassing occasion when he was required to explain why we'd just broken the London-to-Bath Comet. It had galloped gamely for a morning but finally the old wood of the front box gave out and the telegraph spring crashed through. Luckily the gentleman at Dodington House, whose coach it was, took it all very calmly which was just as well for I was wondering where the editor of Nationwide was going to get the money from—original mails I'm told come a bit pricey.

It was by no means our only disaster in the four weeks of filming. On the very first day we managed to perpetrate two others. First, the idiot reporter lost his car keys, and finally had to abandon his car in the middle of a field in Hertfordshire. And while we were scouring the ground for the keys the director contrived to walk, with head bent, straight into a tree. I got the car back two days later. The director got three stitches the same afternoon.

But we didn't let small inconveniences put us off, not even when the director's head had healed and he then contracted tonsillitis, not even when the reporter nearly passed out in the freak heatwaves of June wearing the full Monty Berman Victorian kit, dressed up like an extra from "A Christmas Carol" in ninety-five degrees of heat.

In the end, it *was* all worth it. We saw the grand view of a coach and four opening our series, as the London-to-York mail clattered down Stamford High Street, the coach horn blowing and the church bells ringing out in answer. There were to be sights like that, sights of the great romantic age of coaching throughout our five films. As one who normally spends his life aiming himself like a bullet toward his destination, wondering indeed whether he can make Birmingham before the film crew or before the press conference, I was travelling, for a change, the great and direct coach roads of the land, both as Reporter Young and, more particularly, as Passenger Young. It was a fine and romantic experience.

MARTIN YOUNG
Westcott Barton
1976

Filming of *Stagecoach*

The making of the film *Stagecoach* gave all involved a unique opportunity to look back and see how travellers fared in the days when travel was an adventure. Alan Scales, the producer, assembled his crew at Knebworth House on June 7 1976. Martin Young brought along his bicycle which was to feature so prominently in the film carrying the self-styled Passenger Young across England, tracing the great coach roads and the development of an unparalleled system of transport.

The stars of the show were to be a unique collection of coaches located by the Nationwide researchers and they included three mail coaches and four road coaches. Four teams of horses were used in the filming and were made available by George Mossman, of Luton, Major Simon Codrington, of Dodington, Tom Parker, of Droxford, and me.

The opening shots are of the York mail, and Passenger Young is now on the London to York road and he stops to take refreshment on the twenty-hour journey at the George Hotel, Stamford.

The George itself had been an important staging post for 250 years, until the A1 by-passed it in 1960. As the roar of the traffic rumbled away, Stamford and the George won back their old world atmosphere, until today you would hardly think anything had changed at all. Even the original coach waiting rooms are here—the Down waiting room for York passengers and the Up waiting room for London passengers. One always went Up to London.

Back in 1706 forty coaches a day passed through these archways—twenty up and twenty down. The fare was twenty-five shillings on the inside, and fifteen shillings if you were prepared to brave the elements and sit outside. By 1830 Passenger Young was suffering from a hundred years of inflation. He would be paying three pounds ten shillings for the ten-hour trip to London!

Peter Munt driving the York Mail into the yard of the George Hotel, Stamford.

From Stamford the scene moved to the Heycock Inn, Wansford, and thence on to Stilton some fourteen miles down the road where we came to the beautiful Bell Inn. There is not much to stop for in Stilton these days, except for the Bell's Tudor façade sagging under its weight of history. James White, restaurant manager for London's Hilton Hotel, has just bought the crumbling elegance of the Bell. Over the next five years he plans to restore it as a place of fine hospitality and retirement.

Here Passenger Young recalls the comments of passengers on the road. "I sat nearest the wheel, and the moment we set off I fancied I saw certain death before me." . . . "The machine rolled along with prodigious rapidity . . . and every moment we seemed to fly into the air, so much so that it appeared to me a complete miracle that we stuck to the coach at all."

But surprisingly, after all that, most modern-day coach travellers are delighted with the comfort of the ride. It is the first thing they remark on, but we forget that our roads are solid and level. Once you get onto rougher ground you realise how excruciating a thirty-hour coach trip must have been, particularly since in those thirty hours you stopped for just forty minutes. No wonder the early coach travellers used to make their wills out before they set off!

Despite its disrepair, the Bell Inn is still an attractive place and attracts artists like Luke Sykes. Luke is a Huntingdonshire farmer, but his real delight is in coaches and coach travel. As he sketches and paints old inns he enlivens them again with coaches and passengers. The daring and romantic old coaches clatter through his work—the Tally-Ho, Telegraph, Antelope, Confederate, Celebrity, Royal Express, the Union Balloon. When Luke is not in his studio painting coaches, he is often travelling as one of the few guards in the land. What more amiable passenger than Luke Sykes as he travels the old coach routes with Passenger Young.

Luke taught himself to blow a coaching horn and his calls punctuate the film. The unlovely blast of a car horn is the most musical sound you would hear today on the A1. Today's motor coaches flash by at seven times the speed, never noticing the memorials to an earlier age that still stand mile after mile. In about six hour's time Passenger Young was in London, ready to take a welcome rest after his twenty-hours marathon from York.

The stable yard at Hotham Hall.

Right
The passengers stretch their legs while filming at Hotham Hall in Humberside.

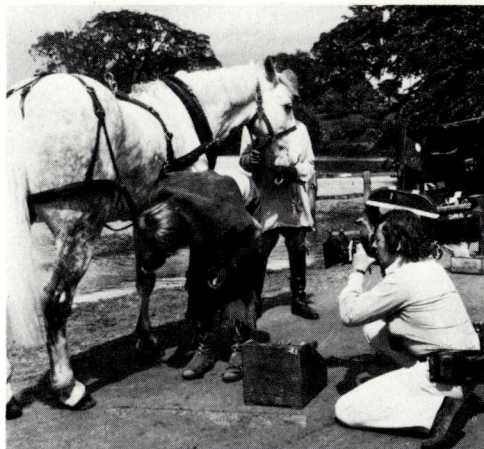

Right
A new shoe for Merlin while filming at Gawsworth.

Far right
John Richards drives his team to the Holyhead mail before the Nationwide camera in the fields near Gawsworth Hall.

Hotham Hall, the home of Captain and Mrs Dick Odey, was the scene of the next phase of filming. In these elegant surroundings we were made comfortable and entertained to dinner by our host and hostess. We all stood breathless when we viewed the Devonport Mail silent and still in its coach-house. Quicksilver was the crack mail coach. Hers is the story of time and speed. But for the last fifty years she has stood still in a museum, her agility and dash denied, her ash-wood and axles growing old. So it was both exciting and frightening to put horses to her the following morning, for this was the day we brought the old coach out. The children turned up to watch and to wonder; the old horsemen turned up to watch and remember. It was my task to ease her into action after her long rest, nursing her old joints along the metalled road.

Our next stop was my home, Gawsworth Hall, where the horses were pleased to be back in their own stables. In the tranquil beauty of the historic village we started filming the Holyhead Mail on the road, and took general continuity shots before starting filming a change of horses at the Harrington Arms down the long avenue of limes from the hall.

To give extra effect to the shots the old inn was bathed in artificial light and the lamps of the coach given extra power from an electric circuit connected to a car battery. The sight proved an enormous crowd puller and hundreds of people turned up to see the filming.

We waited for the summer evening to turn to dusk and finally to night. It was not until about 2 30 am that the weary horses trotted up the ancient avenue and past the silent pools back to the stables, the lights from the lamps flickering on the hedgerows. One could see why passengers on the Red Rover of the Golden Age would pay extra to the coachman to deviate half a mile from the main road to see the glories of the village.

9

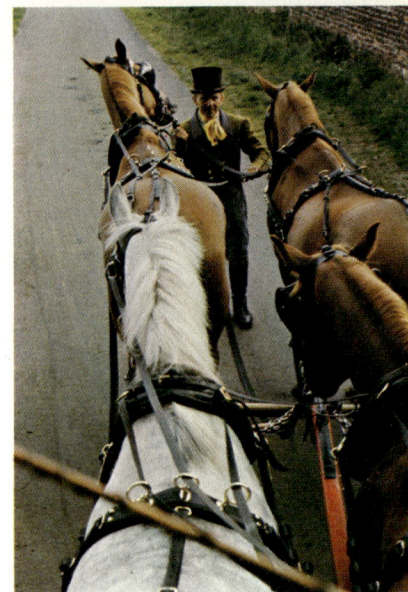

The next day we all slept in and resumed filming after lunch in the fourteen acre field behind the hall—this time of the Sheffield Telegraph which used to run between Sheffield and Buxton in the coaching revival. It was a hot afternoon and the horses were not at their best after a late night coupled with a lot of travelling. In this sequence we dealt with a short driving lesson for beginners and a demonstration of the use of looping the reins when turning. For Passenger Young it was hard going following the coach on his bicycle.

From Gawsworth we moved on to Shropshire and the horses, Goldie, Roger, Zorba and Merlin, found themselves at the Ironbridge Gorge Museum. Here we were able to film the coach passing a reconstructed toll house and make use of one of the original Telford toll gates. From there we moved on through the tortuous roads of central Wales to Bangor and the Menai Straits to film the story of the London to Holyhead roads.

Passenger Young and his travelling companion, "Lady Margaret", in real life the wife of Luke Sykes, our guard, were now en route from London on their most historic journey yet. The year is 1826 and the road they are travelling is the new road to Holyhead, the island of Anglesey and thence to Ireland. How elated and privileged they felt to be thundering down the new road with its fine surface and ingenious engineering. And to stop a while at Woburn, reading Paterson's extended account of the beauties of the ancient abbey.

Soon we were to stop at the Bedford Arms in Woburn village itself where they were to muse on its eventful history, for was it not the case that eleven gentlefolk had perished in a fire here fifty years before in 1780? Since that time waifs and spirits have been seen in the first floor rooms. Doors that have been securely bolted fly open and malevolent beings appear and disappear at will to the noxious accompaniment of smoke and smouldering. Passenger Young was a bit put out in 1830.

But, ghosts apart, the real story of the London-Holyhead run is the story of a road—a fine straight road built by the Romans, nearly two thousand years ago. It lasted for centuries until another great road builder set to work on it. He was a Scottish engineer called Thomas Telford.

The only thing to be said for the state of the old coach roads in the eighteenth century was that it gave rise to some superb vilification. This, for instance, is a 1770 account of the roads: "I know not in the whole range of language terms sufficiently expressive to describe this infernal road." . . . "A thousand and one travellers will break their necks or their limbs by overthrows or breakings down." . . . "I actually measured ruts of four feet deep floating with mud." Another writer complained on a nine-hour coach trip "I suffered between ten thousand and twelve thousand severe contusions."

Top left
Passengers paid extra for a small diversion from the regular route to enjoy the Cheshire countryside.

Top
Passenger Young and Lady Margaret inspect the horses before their journey begins.

Above
A rest for Roger, Goldie, Merlin and Zorba during busy days and nights of filming.

It's now just how Telford left it, except of course for our modern tarmacadam surface. But it's still wide enough and strong enough for today's vast volume of traffic, pounding along at speeds that Telford could not have imagined.

The original dash along the new road was in the cold January of 1826. Fast though it was the London-Holyhead journey still took a whole day and a whole night of horse changes, hurried meals and tankards of rough ale, both horses and victuals being provided by the innkeepers along the way. Another day dawns with still seventy miles to go, but the gradients remain easy, the bridges carry them with speed across the rivers and Holyhead is now but a few hours away. Twenty-two miles from Holyhead stands Telford's greatest single achievement on the London-Holyhead road, the Menai Bridge.

The day we crossed the bridge was a great moment for everyone. The police stopped the traffic in our honour and we all were fully conscious of the great sense of occasion. For me it was the high spot of the filming to drive the actual Holyhead Mail over the famous bridge. The day dawned misty and overcast, but somehow this did not seem to matter and like Telford we drove over four or five times to savour the experience to the full. At this point we said goodbye to the Holyhead Mail and entrusted it to George Almond to drive the Land Rover and trailer with its precious load on the first stage of its journey back to Burton Constable Hall, Hull, where it is on exhibition, and the film crew headed south for Salisbury.

John Richards drives his team on the return journey across the Menai Bridge.

On June 18 Mr Sanders Watney drove the Red Rover through the grounds of Breamore House, Fordingbridge, and filming started on the story of the London to Southampton road. Today Passenger Young is setting out on the seventy-mile trip from London to Southampton. Like the true adventurer he is, he's undaunted by the contusions on his long journey from York, but nonetheless glad that this journey will take him just eight hours in 1830, particularly as he knows from his research that one hundred years before a similar trip would have taken twenty-eight hours.

The Bull at East Sheen is a typical big London inn of the period. At the height of the coaching era it was a noted coaching centre and a beer delivery here in the nineteenth century meant four thousand gallons. So maybe Passenger Young enjoyed a pint or two as he waited for his Red Rover connection to Southampton. His journey began though, like that of so many other people, six miles away at Hyde Park Corner where, in 1830, three hundred coaches a day used to pass. Hyde Park Corner, in fact, trampled by coaches and horses looked much as it does today steamrollered by motor cars.

Passenger Young confides "I confess I am impressed by my nice condescension in travelling outside. It did seem necessary to my writing that I experience not merely the travel habits of a gentleman on the inside, but also the manner by which the common man is conveyed."

One recalls Macready's account of outside travel in 1811: "I go into the coach—its odours were many, varied and unpleasantly mingled, and the passengers, a half drunken sailor and an old woman, did not impress me with the prospect of a very pleasant journey. Most fortunately my travelling companions appear neither malodorous nor inebriated, but one still shudders to think of the perpetual danger one risks perched so precariously atop the coach. Could our coachman stop in time? Could he indeed stop without overturning?"

Indeed the coachman was the tough trend-setter of his day. As one historian wrote "Every ragamuffin that has a coat to his back thrusts his hands into his pockets, rolls his gait, talks slang and is an embryo coachey."

Our coachman, on Red Rover, spurred her on, meanwhile, down the last few miles to Southampton, where Passenger Young was delivered safely. The organisation was impeccable. It did take just eight hours, they changed horses five times and it cost Passenger Young fourteen shillings and sixpence. It leaves him with a purse full of sovereigns as he sets out on the hazardous journey from Bath to London, its rich and elegant road peopled by rich and elegant vagabonds like Claude Duval and Hawkes, the Flying Highwayman.

The scene now changes to Dodington House, Chipping Sodbury, where we are filming with Colin Henderson and the Comet. The coach had been taken out of the carriage museum and after a morning of hard use in the park, the front bearing members collapsed and the springs found themselves in the front boot. It was too much for such a lady of her years but luckily no-one was hurt and the damage easily repaired.

Passenger Young's day on film begins in a private coach as he made his way to Bath to pick up the London-to-Bath Comet and travel the route of elegance. It wasn't always so elegant: back in 1667 when the first Bath Flying Machine was advertised, it took a sweaty and muddy three days to make the trip, if God permit! By 1830 Jane Austen had immortalised the genteel society of Bath and this was the route of high fashion and took just twelve hours.

So the fashionable and the elegant prepare to return to London. Luke Sykes, our by now familiar guard, assists the ladies who are to travel outside, and offers to help Lady Margaret to her seat inside the coach. Lady Margaret is a lady of independent means who has chosen to make the grand tour of the direct roads. What could be more apt as they depart from this proud city than the strutting and crying of a peacock.

Sanders Watney driving the Red Rover at Breamore House in Hampshire.

The Comet in the Dodington Carriage Museum.

The dangers were many, not least from the elements. One seasoned traveller expressed his particular fear "Give me collision, a broken axle, and an overturn, a runaway team, a drunken coachman, snowstorms, howling tempests, but Heaven preserve us from floods".

On now to the wide and busy streets of the market town of Marlborough where thoughts of accidents recur, as twentieth century traffic roars by the vulnerable cyclist. I recognise the feeling of concern, not to say panic, that must have seized Passenger Young from time to time as the Comet galloped along the busy roads. So on to Woolhampton, with memories not of coaching for once but of the railways. The station at Woolhampton is called Midgham because the old Great Western Railway passengers used to think they were travelling to Wolverhampton. Memories too of a fine old coaching inn crowding across the narrow street. Whatever happened to the Angel now that the M4 sweeps by a few miles to the north?

Colin Henderson and the Comet in a hurry at Dodington.

So nearer and nearer to London, nearer in particular to Maidenhead Thicket and Hounslow Heath. Passenger Young remarked "I have heard it mooted that even within the last few years many travellers would consider it quite usual to be robbed at least once in their journey. Indeed most would consider the territory our coachman is about to traverse as the most dangerous in England, with respect to footpads, vagabonds and highwaymen."

This was where the Flying Highwayman, Hawkes, came to grief. It was late one night at the Rising Sun Inn. He had just ridden a hard twenty-five miles from the scene of a particularly daring robbery at Maidenhead Thicket and he was in the middle of his meal, drinking his brandy and relaxing at the end of a long day's thieving, when a fight broke out between two old rustics in smocks. It seemed to be an argument about the beer and Hawkes took no notice until one of the rustics drew a knife and threatened to stab the other. Now Hawkes was a man of quick reflexes and he was over in a flash and was quickly pinioned to the ground and handcuffed. Off came the smocks and Hawkes saw the red tunics of the Bow Street Runners. Hawkes, like so many before him, was to swing from Tyburn Gallows.

But London approaches, and with it more sinister tales. Seventeen miles away from London travellers would take their rest at the Ostrich, Colnbrook. It is reckoned to be the fourth oldest inn in Britain. In coaching days there used to be a flap on the first floor so that outsiders could step straight off the coach into their rooms. But if you were a rich insider then you could get into quite a different sort of flap here at the Ostrich. The landlord, a man called Jarvis, would invite coach travellers with fat purses to stay in his special blue room. When the wealthy incumbent of the room was sleeping the landlord would pull a lever hinging the floor beneath the bed and plunging the gentleman into a vat of boiling liquid down below. Sixty-five people went just that way and as they writhed in the vat Jarvis would go upstairs and steal all their money and then throw the corpses into the nearby river Coln.

14

But even the Ostrich has its elegant links. In the Middle Ages royal visitors would stop here to change into their ceremonial robes before visiting the King at Windsor.

And here is one of the most elegant signs of all of the Bath road, the Bath road pumps. In 1754 Beau Nash, who wanted to promote the city of Bath as a fashionable resort, had water pumps placed at two-mile intervals along the way. He employed roadmen to water the road and lay the dust, so that all the fashionable gentry might arrive clean and tidy to take the waters at Bath.

Even then Hounslow was a key crossroads—the Clapham Junction of coach travel. Today it plays a reluctant host to modern jets taking off and landing at London Heathrow.

By Heathrow standards the Bath road was never busy, yet by 1834 people marvelled that twenty-two coaches a day used to travel it.

The last piece of action to be filmed using coach and horses was at Droxford, with that great character "the Guvner". This is the way everyone addresses Tom Parker, one of the greatest characters that coaching has thrown up in the last decade. Many people have found his ample wit shine through any programme in which he takes part, and television documentaries have chronicled his life and demonstrated how a large farm and dairy business could be built up by a man of vision.

The Guvner had the Rocket ready for us and our history books tell us that the former guard of this coach, Francis Faulkner, lies in a vault in Farlington churchyard and left instructions that the horn was always to be sounded when the coach passed the churchyard.

As well as filming with the Rocket, we met Tom Parker's daughter, Mrs Rusbridger, and we were shown how to put a team of six horses together to a brake.

Tom Parker (the Guvner) and his team of bays to the Rocket.

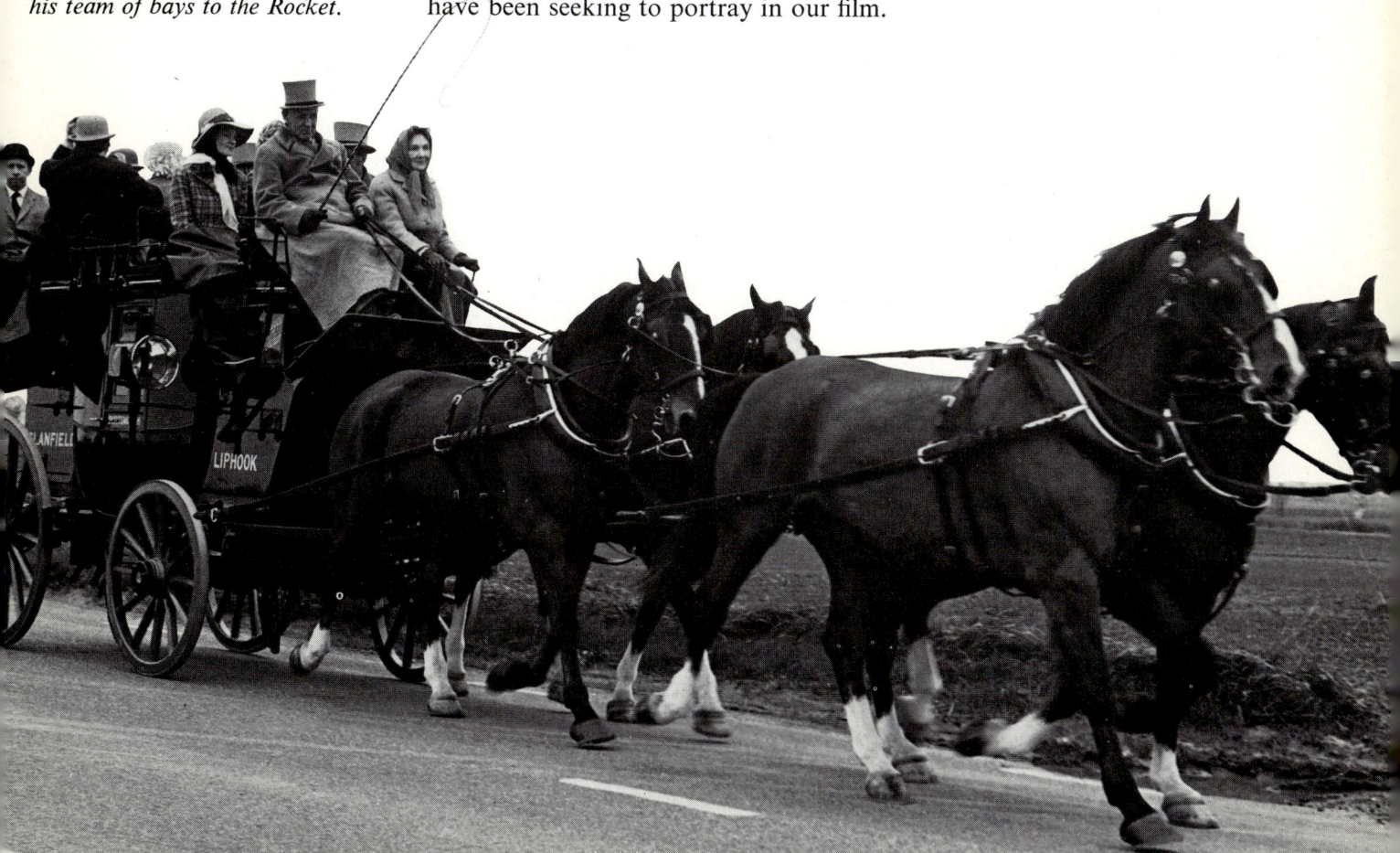

It was fitting that a visit to the Guvner should conclude our filming because he does epitomise the spirit of another generation of coachmen, the people we have been seeking to portray in our film.

YORK Four Days Stage-Coach.

Begins on Friday the 12th of April 1706.

ALL that are desirous to pass from London to York, or from York to London, or any other Place on that Road; Let them Repair to the Black Swan in Holbourn in London, and to the Black Swan in Coney-street in York.

At both which Places, they may be received in a Stage Coach every Monday, Wednesday and Friday, which performs the whole Journey in Four Days, (if God permits.) And sets forth at Five in the Morning.

And returns from York to Stamford in two days, and from Stamford by Huntington to London in two days more. And the like Stages on their return.

Allowing each Passenger 14l, weight, and all above 3d. a Pound.

Performed By ⎰ Benjamin Kingman.
⎱ Henry Harrison,
⎱ Walter Baynes,

Also this gives Notice that Newcastle Stage Coach, sets out from York, every Monday, and Friday, and from Newcastle every Monday, and Friday.

Roed in pt. 05-00. 0 of Mr. Bodingfold for 5
for Monday the 3 of June 1706   7p

Early history

Old Birmingham coaching bill.

In summer— if God permit

The precursor of the stage coach was the stage waggon, an enormous cumbersome vehicle intended for the carriage of large and bulky goods. Its wheels were very broad so that they might be of some help in traversing the muddy tracks which passed for roads. In effect they rolled the sludge into some sort of carriageway which would have defeated the later iron rims which would have immediately sunk into the mud and made further progress impossible. Travel was slow, and if fortunate a speed of two miles per hour was averaged using teams of up to eight horses.

This, therefore, was the method of transport for loads from 1500 until about 1750 when a gradual transformation took place. The new system relied on the same stage waggons but it had one significant development: it changed horses at specified points along the route.

The first glimpse we have of stage coaches was far removed from the spanking coaches of the Golden Age. They were crudely constructed with a wooden body covered in stout leather. There were no doors or windows, only heavy curtains which afforded the traveller some protection from the elements. The body was suspended on huge leather braces and rocked violently, while the coachman and guard sat on an unsprung seat covered by a hammer-cloth. It was not long, however, before windows and doors had become more general, and red had become the generally accepted colour for the wheels and running gear.

It was the period from 1730 onwards which saw the blossoming of trade in Britain and therefore a better network of communication was essential. The towns of the provinces became increasingly aware that they had to have good access to the capital as it was the most important trading centre in the land. Coach proprietors now boldly announced their new "flying machines", and in 1731 Nicholas Rothwell, of Warwick, instigated a service between Birmingham and London. A passenger paid twenty-one shillings and the journey was accomplished in two and a half days "if God permit". Passengers were allowed

Left
Lent to Science Museum, London, by Mr A C Turner.

Right
Leather braces were an early form of suspension, and the box seat was unsprung to ensure that the coachman kept awake.
Photograph, Science Museum, London.

The basket at the rear of this early
coach was intended for luggage
but it was soon adapted for carrying
poor passengers.
Photograph, Science Museum, London.

to carry fourteen pounds of luggage. If they wished to carry more a surcharge of one penny per pound was levied. It is fairly safe to assume that this service ran only in the summer months as conditions were too bad in winter and the roads became impassable with mud.

Much is recorded of the discomforts suffered by travellers in these vehicles. The leather braces allowed the coach to lurch violently in every direction, and it is known that many unfortunate travellers suffered agonies of nausea on the long journeys. Rothwell's crude woodcut advertising his services gives us some idea of how the horses were harnessed. Four horses were driven from the box seat by the coachman and the lead horses were controlled by a postillion riding on the off leader.

In 1754 Manchester and London were at last in direct communication. The journey of 182 miles was accomplished in four and a half days. The Liverpool Flying Machine was on the road some four years later and offered stiff competition by covering the 206 miles in three days. The fare was two guineas, which worked out at approximately tuppence-halfpenny per mile.

Stage coaches now were equipped with what was called a "conveniency behind", in essence a basket hung on the back by two huge leather straps. Originally it was intended to carry the luggage but it was soon adapted as a cheap way of carrying passengers. These unfortunate travellers have been immortalised for all time by Hogarth in his picture of a stage coach in an inn yard.

By 1774 steel springs had been announced by the London and Shrewsbury coach. It also boasted "bows on the top" which presumably meant iron rails for the safety of the passengers, as it was not unknown for those riding on the roof seats to be thrown off.

It was during the last decade of the eighteenth century that stage coaches, with which we are now generally familiar, were developed. Front and hind boots on the coaches gave the outside passengers a more secure foothold. The rough and ready outside passengers, often laughing and joking on the roof seats, upset the more delicate thoughts of those travelling inside. Coaches were now fitted with springs under the box seats thanks to John Warde. This move had been resisted in case the smoother ride resulted in the coachman dozing off to sleep, but it was soon demonstrated that a more comfortable coachman could drive longer distances, which naturally pleased the proprietors.

Shorter stages of some ten miles enabled coaches to maintain a hitherto unheard of speed. The main routes to the provinces became subject to fierce competition, and what better medium for proclaiming their virtues than the coaches themselves? They adopted smart and often gaudy liveries and assumed names such as Wonder, Telegraph and Tally-Ho. They were lettered on their front and hind boots with their destinations and stopping places and often looked very flashy when compared with the simple impressive dignity of the mail coaches.

Standards of efficiency improved beyond recognition, and the country was now poised on the brink of an enormous explosion which was to revolutionise travel in Britain so that it became the envy of the world.

John Palmer

The son of a wealthy brewer, John Palmer was intended for the church. But this was not to be and he entered into the management of his father's theatres. In his quest for performers he travelled the country and felt the service then offered by the postboys was less than adequate. It was Palmer's dream that a network of mail coaches be set up to cover the kingdom. The main plank for his argument was that the mail coaches would cost no more than the postboy system. He would never have succeeded in his bold plan without the enthusiastic support of Pitt against the antagonistic officials of the Post Office who never forgave this outsider for interfering in their domain.

The network was to be paid for by private finance and the Post Office would pay threepence a mile—the same as the postboys. The mail coaches were to be exempted from the onerous turnpike charges and allowed to carry paying passengers.

On Monday August 2 1784 the first of Palmer's mails started its journey from Bristol, through Bath to London. Such was its success that the system spread with great rapidity. Punctual, efficient and amazingly well organised, it was a revolution. Within fifty years mail coaches covered twelve thousand miles of Britain every night.

Palmer knew what he was doing and he was no head-in-the-clouds dreamer. He dearly wanted success and above all recognition and position. Naturally he was delighted when, in October 1786, he was appointed Comptroller General, a position of considerable influence. In addition he was paid a handsome salary and a percentage of Post Office revenue which was to swell his already not inconsiderable fortune.

By 1787 Palmer's fame had spread across the channel, and negotiations were started with the French Minister of Posts to see whether a system based on this concept could be adopted in France. Negotiations were still taking place when his dream of an integrated and efficient transport system in Europe had to be abandoned because of the French revolution.

At the same time, a contemporary German writer, Joachim Campe, complained that owing to the high speed he saw nothing of the countryside while travelling from Yarmouth to London. Palmer no doubt took this complaint as an accolade from a foreigner envious of the system he had devised and nurtured.

By 1797 there were forty-two mail coaches established in Britain with 4 110 miles of the countryside covered. The mails had already demonstrated that they were a considerable saving in cost over the amount previously paid to the post-boys. The total service now cost the department £12 416 a year as opposed to around double that amount previously.

Palmer had also made a valuable contribution to the cause of true love. He had enabled a lady and her beau from London to be at Gretna Green in Scotland before her father had time to know what had happened and set off in pursuit of the lovers.

Palmer: a man with a vision of a countrywide mail coach system.
By courtesy of the Post Office

Twelve thousand miles

Not everyone, however, approved of such high-speed travel and many were convinced it was bad for their health and "detrimental to the human brain", causing sudden death.

At the age of 50 his enemies in the Post Office engineered his dismissal but again with Pitt's help he retained a pension of some £3 000 a year.

Palmer's achievements did not go unrecorded. Mail coach halfpennies were struck in his honour, and one bears the date 1797. The inscription on the reverse side reads "To J. Palmer, Esq. This Is Inscribed as a Token of Gratitude for Benefits Received from the Establishment of Mail Coaches". Gainsborough painted his portrait and he received the freedom of eighteen cities to whom he had helped bring prosperity. He represented Bath in Parliament from 1801–1807, and he died in Brighton in 1818. He was laid to rest in the Abbey Church, Bath.

The original Bath mail coach.
By courtesy of the Post Office

THE *ORIGINAL* BATH MAIL COACH.
Invented by M. Palmer at Bath, and Supported by GOVERNMENT.

The mail coaches

The mail coach system was the pride of Britain and the envy of the world. These splendid coaches were painted in a livery of red, maroon and black. On each of the quarter panels appeared the stars of the four Great Orders of Knighthood, namely the Garter, Thistle, Bath and St Patrick. The upper panels of the body were black together with the fore and hind boots. In contrast, the royal cipher was picked out in gold on the fore boot, and the number on the hind. The royal arms were emblazoned on the door panels which were in a deep maroon. The running gear and wheels were Post Office red. They were indeed the undoubted kings of the road: they paid no tolls, ran untaxed, and claimed right of way over all transport.

The guard sat on a small round seat at the rear of the coach. A bearskin covering was provided to help resist the worst of the cold, although this was

By courtesy of the Post Office

ROYAL MAILS, STARTING FROM THE POST OFFICE, LOMBARD STREET.

THIS PLATE Engraved by Charles Hunt from an Original picture by J. J. E. Jones is respectfully Dedicated to the Proprietors of the Royal Mail

The Holyhead mail, one of the few surviving mail coaches.

Above right
The York mail passes a toll gate at night.
By courtesy of the Post Office

not standard, and sheepskin or tiger skins were also used. To gain access to the mail the guard had to be dislodged from his seat, and he spent the journey firmly presiding over the hinged door to the hind boot. Attached to the coach roof was his weapon case which was in easy reach in case of attack. Close at hand was his "yard of tin" or horn on which he would imperiously blow "Clear the road" or one of many established calls.

In the early part of the nineteenth century it was decided that all mail coaches be constructed to a uniform pattern. This in effect was a far-reaching decision. It was the beginning of mass production to a high standard. Parts were held in stock and were interchangeable so that in case of an accident or other misfortune the mails could be repaired easily and be on the road again quickly.

The coaches were made by Vidler who had the contract from the Post Office from 1784 to 1836. The original design was so good that, apart from minor

The York mail leaves the Old Bell at Stilton.

alterations to the perch* and springing, their construction remained virtually unchanged. The early mails had straight perches which made them high with a high centre of gravity. The result was a certain instability and hence they were potentially dangerous. Consequently the perch was curved downward to accommodate the body, thus lowering the centre of gravity and making a positive contribution to safety. To ensure further steady running, the length of the perch was fixed at not less than six feet which was the minimum allowed by the Post Office. A short-coupled coach was found to rock unpleasantly at speed.

In early vehicles the wheels were kept in place by primitive linch pins which were a constant source of accidents. The introduction of the mail axle was a great step forward as the wheel was secured by three bolts which made the shedding of a wheel almost impossible. For ease of lubrication, the later mails had patent oil boxes which eliminated the time-wasting process of removing the wheels.

As much of the journey was by night, the mails carried ample lamps. The main lamps were set in reversible cases so that by day the glass could be protected from stones or other dangers. Hung on the footboard above the wheelers was a footboard lamp to throw light on the horses' backs and harness. In fog it was found that the light would reflect back in the coachman's eyes so to help counteract this problem a thick piece of leather was kept by the guard which could be strapped over half the glass. This worked in the same way as a car's dipped headlights.

Until 1829 all the mails left from the General Post Office in Lombard Street. This was a cramped and unworthy site, however, and the new building at St Martins-le-Grand was an impressive backcloth for the renowned spectacle of the mail coaches leaving at 8 o'clock. The northern coaches rumbled down Aldersgate Street and the southern ones by Cheapside. During the day they had been inspected and cleaned before their journey, and every detail had been checked by an official inspector. From here the Holyhead Mail set out on its 260-mile journey which it was to cover in under twenty-seven hours. This included an allowance of forty minutes for meals and stops for twenty-seven changes of horses.

In complete contrast the arrival of the incoming mails was not nearly as glamorous a spectacle. They would start arriving in the small hours of the morning with the foam flecked horses proof of their speed through the night. Dusty and dishevelled passengers would dismount and fatigued horses would be lead away to rest their well-tested sinews.

Once a year from 1791 a parade of mail coaches was held in honour of the King's birthday. Thousands of spectators lined the route from Vidler's factory in Millbank where the coaches were lined up in new paint with their teams of dashing horses. Each coach carried a colourful hammer-cloth for the parade, and there was much competition to ride inside the coaches. The Bristol Mail lead the others in order of seniority on the road, and the guards wore their scarlet coats and new gold-laced hats. The route they took varied but they always went by way of the home of the Postmaster General, St James Palace and the General Post Office, until this custom lapsed in 1838 when the diminished ranks of the mails gave way to the "iron road".

*perch – a wooden beam connecting front and rear axles.

The kings of the road

Mail coach lamps were reversed in their cases to protect the glass during daytime travel.

Right
The original of this time bill of 1797 is at the Bruce Castle Museum.
By courtesy of the Post Office

The principal proprietors of long-distance stage and Royal Mail coaches from and to London with the number of coaches on lease or owned and the principal coaching establishments.

William James Chaplin (106)
  Swan with Two Necks, Lad Lane
  Spread Eagle, Gracechurch Street
  White Horse, Fetter Lane
Benjamin Worthy Horne (92)
  Golden Cross, Charing Cross
  Cross Keys, Wood Street
  George & Blue Boar, Holborn
  The Bull, Holborn
  Old Bell, Holborn
Edward Sherman (77)
  Bull & Mouth, St Martin's-le-Grand
Robert Nelson (53)
  Belle Sauvage, Ludgate Hill
Robert Gray (29)
  Bolt in Tun, Fleet Street
Robert Fagg (28)
  Bell & Crown, Holborn
  White Bear, Basinghall Street
John Nelson (23)
  The Bull, Aldgate
Sarah Ann Mountain (21)
  Saracens Head, Snow Hill
William Gilbert (21)
  Blossoms Inn, Lawrence Lane
James Hearn (16)
  Kings Arms, Snow Hill

Number of daily departures of long-distance stage and Royal Mail coaches from principal establishments in London

Bull & Mouth, St Martin's-le-Grand	30
Belle Sauvage, Ludgate Hill	29
Golden Cross, Charing Cross	28
Spread Eagle, Gracechurch Street	26
Swan with Two Necks, Lad Lane	23
Bolt in Tun, Fleet Street	20
The Bull, Aldgate	16
The Bull, Holborn	11
George & Blue Boar, Holborn	11
White Horse, Fetter Lane	11
Cross Keys, Wood Street	10
Kings Arms, Snow Hill	10
Blossoms Inn, Lawrence Lane	9
Bell & Crown, Holborn	7
Old Bell, Holborn	7
Saracens Head, Snow Hill	6
White Bear, Basinghall Street	5
	259

NOTES
(a) Total number of coaches leaving London for country places each day: 342
(b) Figures apply to weekdays. Departures considerably reduced on Sundays.

General Post-Office.

The Earl of CHESTERFIELD,
AND
The Earl of LEICESTER,
} Postmaster-General.

London to Exeter Time-Bill.

	Miles	Time allowed H. M.	
			Dispatched from the General Post-Office, the of 179 at
			Coach No sent out { With a Time-Piece safe No to
			Arrived at the Gloucester Coffee-house, Piccadilly, at
Wilson	37½	3 55	Arrived at Bagshot at *11.55*
Demezy	20	2 30	Arrived at Basingstoke at *2.25*
W. Wilson	8½	1 10	Arrived at Overton at *3.35*
Weeks	28½	3 40	Arrived at Salisbury at *7.15*
			Delivered the Time-Piece safe to
			Coach No gone forward
		.30	To be at Salisbury by a Quarter past Seven, where Thirty Minutes are allowed for Breakfast
Shergold	10	1 20	Arrived at Woodyeats at *9.5*
Wood	12½	1 40	Arrived at Blandford at *10.45*
Bryer	16	2 10	Arrived at Dorchester at *12.55*
		30	Thirty Minutes allowed for Dinner, &c.
Warre	27½	4 0	Arrived at Axminster at *5.25*
Pine	9½	1 15	Arrived at Honiton at *6.40*
Land	16	2 10	Arrived at the Post-Office, Exeter, the of 179 at
	179	24 50	The Mail to be delivered at the Post-Office, Exeter, Fifty Minutes past Eight in the Evening
			Coach No arrived { Delivered the Time-Piece safe No to

THE Time of working each Stage is to be reckoned from the Coach's Arrival. Five Minutes for changing four Horses, is as much as is necessary, and as the Time whether more or less, is to be fetched up in the Course of the Stage, it is the Coachman's Duty to be as expeditious as possible, and to report the Horse-keepers if they are not always ready when the Coach arrives, and active in getting it off.

By Command of the Postmaster-General,
T. HASKER.

The mail guards

The first mail guards were the employees of the contractors who furnished the horses. This arrangement proved most unsatisfactory because of the unreliable nature of some of the untrained staff provided on a purely business basis. The Post Office therefore stepped in to take over the appointment of guards so that they became directly responsible to the Crown.

They were given a new and exalted status and were responsible for the time-keeping of the coach and the safe delivery of the mails. In general they were recruited from the army because of their ability to use firearms and to defend the coach and its passengers against the perils of the road. They were also considered to be suitable in terms of reliability and self-resourcefulness gained in service life. They wore scarlet livery to signify their royal appointment as custodians of His Majesty's Mails and they were issued with a blunderbuss to protect the mails, together with a brace of pistols and a cutlass carried in a case. In addition they carried a watch in a sealed case to avoid it being tampered with and this was carried in the leather pouch hung over the shoulder.

The guards often carelessly discharged the blunderbuss to the alarm of passengers and bystanders in general. Things became so bad that an Act of Parliament was passed in 1811 forbidding the firing of a guard's blunderbuss except in defence and instituted a penalty of £5 for the offence.

The guard was provided with an assortment of tools and spare parts so that urgent repairs could be made in the event of a breakdown. He was required to ride on to the next stage with the mails if the coach could go no further on account of an enforced stop, the weather or an accident. It was in the interest of the guard that his coachman should keep to time as a considerable fine was levied if the mail coach was late.

He was the man who often bore the first news, good or bad, into village communities, and he was often not averse to writing a few words for the local newspaper to add to his income of half a sovereign a week. Out of this small sum he had to pay for the oil for his hand lamp and the stable boy who cleaned and reloaded his weapons.

He made up his income where he could and on a main road where the coach was usually full he could expect a tip of two shillings and sixpence from inside passengers and two shillings from the outsiders, which enabled him to enjoy an income of between £300 to £500 a year.

Some of the guards became involved with the illicit trade in game, the sale of which was prohibited before 1831, safe in the knowledge that no one dare challenge or search the Royal Mail. Needless to say this infuriated the country landowners who were unable to do anything to put a stop to the abuse. Thomas Hasker, Chief Superintendent of Mail Coaches, was forced to step in and issue a notice to the effect that local superintendents had the power to search the coach at will and carry out a thorough inspection. In more lighthearted vein he added that he could only permit "such a thing as a turtle tied to the roof, directed to any gentleman to pass unnoticed once or twice during the course of the year but for a constancy cannot be suffered".

The guard was also strictly forbidden to allow any passengers to travel on the hind part of the coach, which offence was punishable by instant dismissal. A

With the waybill pouch over his shoulder, Luke Sykes wears his traditional guard's uniform.

Livery and a blunderbuss

Top left
Quicksilver, the Devonport mail.

Left
The man in the post office window passes a bag of mail to the guard without the Bath mail having to stop.
By courtesy of the Post Office

No. I.—THE START.

PIANOFORTE.

No. II.—CLEAR THE ROAD.

PIANOFORTE.

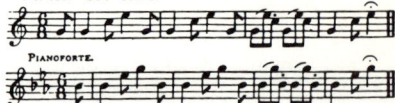

No. III.—OFF SIDE.

PIANOFORTE.

No. IV.—NEAR SIDE.

PIANOFORTE.

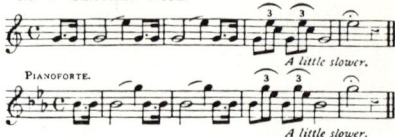

No. V.—SLACKEN PACE.

PIANOFORTE.

No. VI.—PULL UP.

PIANOFORTE.

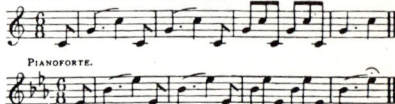

No. VII.—CHANGE HORSES.

PIANOFORTE.

No. VIII.—THE POST-HORN CALL.

PIANOFORTE.

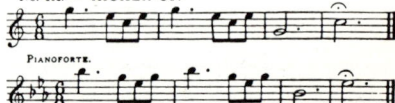

No. IX.—"HIGHER UP."

PIANOFORTE.

No. X.—A RUSTIC CALL.

PIANOFORTE.

No. XI.—"STEADY."

PIANOFORTE.

No. XII.—HOME.

PIANOFORTE.

fine of £5 was payable for permitting an extra passenger on the forward-facing roof seat. It was a lonely vigil for the guard who went the whole distance with the mail coach and was on duty for up to fifteen hours at a spell. Usually he rested the following day when he was able to look after the private commissions he had discreetly undertaken to perform.

The latter part of the coaching era threw up guards whose particular talents were, above all, musical. As well as being experts on the yard of tin they now had a new and more versatile instrument, the key bugle. This was banned by the Post Office as being far too frivolous. It did not, however, stop its use. Guards would buy their own instruments and entertain their passengers while travelling the roads of the country when the coach had cleared the busy streets.

The title of "Last of the Mail Guards" belonged to Moses James Nobbs. He was born in Norwich in 1817 and became guard on the London and Stroud Mail in 1836. In succeeding years he was to be guard on the Exeter and Cheltenham and Aberystwyth Mails which survived the challenge of the railways until 1854. Some of his greatest ordeals were on the remote Welsh roads where snow was the old enemy.

On one occasion his coach was buried in a snow drift between Gloucester and Radnor Forest. His story of heroism and devotion to duty in getting the mail bags to Aberystwyth is well documented, but suffice to say that when he arrived after fifty hours of struggling he was close to death from exposure and exhaustion.

When the Cheltenham and Aberystwyth Mail came off the road in 1854 he was fortunate to find a new position as travelling inspector to the Post Office on the Great Western Railway until his retirement in 1891. He became the elder statesman of his calling, the epitome of all the mails stood for. He died in 1897.

The General Post Office East and the Bull & Mouth Inn, London, painted by James Pollard. By courtesy of the Post Office

Chaplin

At the zenith of his success in 1838, Chaplin had some sixty-eight coaches and 1 800 horses on the roads of Britain and it was reputed he had a turnover of some half a million pounds. At present day values he must have been immensely rich. Coaching was a desperately hard business and many were ruined. It was dominated by a small number of highly successful men who were head and shoulders above their rivals.

Chaplin's roots were firmly planted by the turnpike. He was born at Rochester in 1787, the son of a coachman, who also had stables on the Dover road. He owed much of his success to his early experience gained with his father in both driving and buying horses, and he soon took over the Swan with Two Necks in Lad Lane. From here and other yards throughout London his coaches fanned out in every direction. He was well aware that a dishonest penny was earned by the coachman and guard but he was clever enough to disregard it because if it had been stamped out he would have had to pay higher wages. This practice was known as "shouldering the fares" and "swallowing" of passengers, and it was only when takings did not reach an accepted average that Chaplin would institute an enquiry.

Below
Royal mails prepare to start for the west of England from the yard of the Swan with Two Necks, Lad Lane, Cheapside, London.
By courtesy of the Post Office

From road to railway

Chaplin interested himself in every aspect of his business and worked prodigiously hard. He employed nearly two thousand people and became a legend on account of his uncanny grasp of even the smallest details of his business.

Not content with a major share in some of the most profitable routes, Chaplin established omnibuses to carry passengers to join the coaches and arranged collection of the mail from the General Post Office. Half the mail coaches leaving London were horsed by Chaplin's spanking teams and he proudly enabled the famed Quicksilver to maintain its furious pace across the land. His famous colours of red and black were the livery of many crack coaches, including the Manchester Defiance, Birmingham Greyhound and Bristol Emerald which started their journeys by negotiating the notoriously difficult passageway into Lad Lane and thence to far-away destinations. Most of the horses had been purchased at Horncastle fair, and were accommodated in large underground stables at the Swan with Two Necks.

When many of his competitors could not see the writing on the wall, Chaplin was aware that coaching days were numbered. In association with Benjamin Worthing Horne, he agreed to withdraw competition to certain newly constructed railways, and in return he was able to pick up the lucrative parcel trade between intermediate stations. He then speedily sold his coaches to those reckless enough to invest their money on the recommendation of the previous high takings of his ventures. With his money safely in the bank, he retired for six weeks to Switzerland to contemplate his future.

He now saw clearly that transport would rest with the railways, and accordingly he invested heavily in the new London to Southampton line. It proved a great success and soon he was making more money from steam than he had from the years spent in Lad Lane. He remained as chairman of the new railway for twenty-four years, and he invested in railway projects abroad. Finally, he accepted the accolade of becoming Member of Parliament for Salisbury and died in 1859 in his seventy-second year.

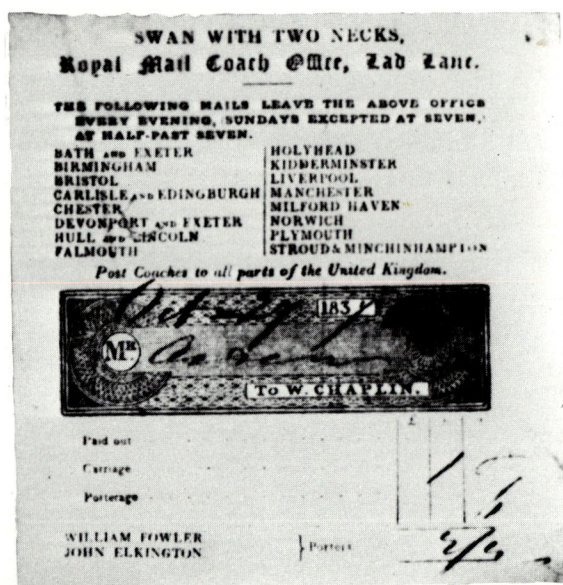

A mail coach ticket.
By courtesy of the Post Office

Turnpike trusts

The roads of England had been neglected since Roman times, and it had become accepted that village communities were responsible for their upkeep. This was an onerous task and was unpopular as magistrates had the power to fine parishes who were neglectful of their responsibilities. As early as 1555 the parliament of Mary Tudor had issued a statute for mending the roads, stating that every parishioner had to spend four days a year maintaining the highway.

As trade grew, it was essential to improve communications, so parliament decided to levy a tax on road users. From 1766 onwards, a series of Turnpike Acts was passed, and special reference was made to the width of waggon wheels, generally accepted as sixteen inches. Not everyone thought the introduction of tolls a good idea and frequently the traveller would be required to pay several tolls to turnpike trusts on a relatively short journey. Daniel Defoe was of a different mind and considered the advantages greatly outweighed the disadvantages and commented "the benefit of a good road abundantly making amends for that little charge".

With the advent of the mail and stage coaches, however, a new situation developed which was of grave concern to the trusts who complained that they lost revenue as the mails passed free of toll and contributed nothing to the upkeep of the roads. It was also pointed out that in some cases the stage coaches had ceased to run as they could not compete with the mails, and revenue was lost in consequence. This was a serious matter for investors as turnpike trust bonds had been considered a safe and profitable investment.

In 1810 the trusts approached parliament but nothing was done and the mails continued to pass freely. In some cases it resulted in the local Turnpike Acts lapsing and investors being ruined. But generally the roads had improved out of all recognition and the more farsighted trusts engaged men like Telford and Macadam as surveyors and who were responsible for the introduction of new scientific processes of road making on an unheard of scale.

Suppertime for the toll-house keeper.

The toll house and a distinctive Telford toll gate.

John Richards drives the Holyhead mail past Telford's reconstructed toll house at Iron bridge.

Telford used a uniform style of tollgate for his great Holyhead Road and many
of the toll houses can still be seen. In general the more sophisticated ones had
projecting eaves so that tolls could be collected without the toll keeper being
soaked on rainy days. They were sited on straight stretches of road to afford a
clear view of oncoming traffic and a remarkable story is told about one particular gate on the Holyhead road. It concerned John Mytton, Squire of Halston in
Shropshire, and has its place in the history of the road as chronicled by Nimrod.

Mytton was a wild young man who, in his more sober moments, had driven a
few stages of the Holyhead Royal Mail without apparent mishap. On one occasion a Shropshire horse dealer called Clarke had brought some horses for Mytton
to try. He ordered his groom to put them together as a tandem and they set off
along the road to see how they went. Obviously impressed, Mytton asked the
dealer whether the lead horse was a good jumper and, on not getting a satis-
factory reply, he determined to find out for himself.

Galloping the horses at a turnpike gate, the leader jumped it in good style,
leaving the two men in their smashed gig with the wheeler still at the gate to the
amazement of the toll keeper.

Luckily such incidents were rare but the toll keeper often had to endure much
abuse in collecting tolls. He also slept at his peril. The guard would herald the
arrival of a mail coach on his horn while some distance away. If the gate was
not open for the passage of the coach, the penalty levied on the unfortunate
offender was forty shillings.

In Ireland, mail coaches had paid toll from 1798, but in Scotland an Act passed
in 1813 made them liable to pay full toll. The Post Office was swift to counter
by putting an extra halfpenny on each letter bound for Scotland. The trusts
cashed in by raising the tolls for the mail coaches, but they were soon brought
to heel when the department took some mails off the road. The victory belonged
to the Post Office.

A tax on the road users

32

Thomas Telford

A road smooth and durable

Thomas Telford was born in Eskdale, Dumfriesshire, the son of a border shepherd who died at the age of 33 only months after the young Thomas was born. Life was hard, but he was fortunate in having an uncle who was able to find the fees for him to attend the small parish school at Westerkirk. When he left he was apprenticed to Andrew Thompson, a master mason in Langholm.

Much of the work he was to undertake was important in giving him practical experience on which he could draw in future years. He was involved in an ambitious programme of road and bridge building on the Duke of Buccleuch's estate, and in 1780 he left Langholm and worked in Edinburgh for twelve months before leaving to seek fame and fortune in London.

He remained in London for six years, working on the theory and practice of engineering and associated subjects that qualified him for his new position of Official Roads Surveyor for Shropshire. He set about a programme of road building and bridge building with enormous gusto. Having proved his point in Shropshire, despite great opposition from vested interests, including the Turnpike Trusts, he turned his attentions to the Scottish Highlands.

The government made him responsible for a far reaching scheme of road building and for the construction of ports to serve the Scottish fishing industry. His most challenging task, however, was still to come, and he was soon requested to reconstruct the important London to Holyhead artery. Work was begun in 1815 and was not completed until 1829.

The cost of a Telford road was around £1 000 per mile. For this great sum a road of unparalleled smoothness and durability was guaranteed and every section was meticulously surveyed and inspected by Telford. The bed of the road was carefully graded with a slope from the crown to the sides to ensure good drainage. On this base a layer of stones, some seven to ten inches deep was laid, and above this was a layer of hard stone chippings. This was then compounded with a steam or horse roller, and under the rolling of the traffic the angular stones locked to a solid mass.

As a prelude to his greater work he completed a single span bridge at Bettws-y-Coed in 1817. This was cast by William Hazledine and is known as the Waterloo Bridge. It proudly boasts this inscription "This arch was constructed in the same year the Battle of Waterloo was fought", and clearly Telford recognised this event as the most significant of the period.

Soon the Irish Members of Parliament and their fellow travellers were able to journey with unparalleled speed on the new roads which boasted no gradient of more than one in twenty-two. With the Act of Union which allowed Irish MPs to sit at Westminster, the route became politically important. By 1819 work on the road had reached a feverish pitch and the mail coaches were able to pass with speed and safety to Bangor. It was at a spot known locally as Pig Island that work began on Telford's greatest single achievement on the Holyhead road —the suspension bridge over the Menai Straits linking the mainland with the island of Anglesey.

No major engineering work in history could have been unveiled with less ceremony. After all, this was the largest bridge to be built in Britain and its opening was of national importance.

Telford recorded "At half past one o'clock the London mail coach first passed over the estuary, at the level of a hundred feet above that tideway which heretofore has presented a decisive obstruction to travellers."

The date was January 30 1826. The coachman was David Davies and the guard was William Read, and it was these men, together with the mail coach superintendent Mr Aker, and as many as could climb aboard the coach, who opened the bridge. It was a stormy night and the wind moaned in the girders and chains as the waters restlessly churned below. Sperm oil lanterns lighted the carriage way and the whole effect was eerie as, in the gathering storm, the coach passed over on its first journey.

In the morning, despite torrential rain, a procession of coaches, carriages and humble carts crossed the new bridge. In the first carriage rode one of the commissioners, A E Fuller, followed by Telford and Sir Henry Parnell. After them came three coaches, the Caernarvon day coach, the Bangor stage coach, Pilot, and the London stage coach, the Oxonian. At noon the weather cleared and the local population wondered at the triumph of engineering that had been built on their soil. The road to Ireland was open.

John Richards drives his team on their historic journey a hundred and fifty years after the opening of the Menai Bridge.

It was with enormous pride and a great feeling of occasion that exactly one hundred and fifty years later I was to climb onto the box of the London to Holyhead Mail and drive my team over the bridge. It is possible that the coach could have been the actual one used that stormy night so many years ago. Momentarily the leaders faltered as they saw the water so far below and the steelwork of the bridge rising high above them, but they seemed to have a sense of occasion and trotted boldly on to the span which quivered with their approaching hoofbeats.

A mist hung over the bridge, and a fine rain came out of an overcast sky. Perhaps it was a sign that the elements had now half-accepted this colossus that spanned the Straits, as we were spared the tempest of that first day so many years ago.

Though travel was often hard, passengers saw the beauty of rural England.

34

The coach horse

In 1835 over seven hundred mail coaches were on the roads of Britain. Most of the fast ones averaged ten miles an hour and some considerably more. To maintain this furious pace, good-quality horses were needed and great care was taken in their choosing.

The cost of the horses, on average, was £25 to £30 and their useful life on the road was four years. In general a horse was expected to do his stage every day, excepting every fourth day when he was rested. The distance of the stage varied according to conditions but it was usually around ten miles. In large towns, a beautifully matched team would be used so that they proclaimed the speed, elegance and panache with which they would complete their journey. On the rural stages not nearly so much trouble was taken and the teams lacked the excellence in turnout and matching of their urban counterparts.

Many of these horses were bought cheaply because they had proved unmanageable in private hands. Hard work in a team, however, soon brought them to heel and even the most vicious found they needed all their energy to survive on long, hard stages. Often unscrupulous proprietors obtained horses by dishonest means and these were used at night when they would not be recognised.

They were sold when they became unsound in wind or limb or had just lost the spark to gallop at the speed required. These animals were sold to eager purchasers who would often get years of good service from them doing less glamorous tasks. It was always the case, however, of *caveat emptor* when dealing with the legendary Hobson who would allow no choosing of horses. You took the next in line and liked it. Hobson's choice in fact!

Very often coachmen liked to drink and converse at the changes and therefore had to make up time at the expense of their unfortunate horses. To spur their teams to great feats of exertion they used a whip similar to the cat-o-nine-tails which was known as the "apprentice" or the "short Tommy". Chaplin had a strict rule that any of his coachmen using this instrument of torture would be dismissed at once.

The horses of the Exeter-London mail coach impatient for the off.
By courtesy of the Post Office

In town and country

Left
Peter Munt drives the York Mail out of Stamford.

Right
The coachman of the Bath Mail chats to his solitary passenger.
By courtesy of the Post Office

The York Mail. Only on the country stages were the horses not matched for colour.
By courtesy of the Post Office

At night it was something of a nightmare for both coachmen and horses as under cover of darkness on some roads the lame and the blind were put to work. Here in conditions of abject misery they were forced to spend the last remaining months of their existence working at a time when no member of the public would be able to see their plight.

On the occasions when the night coach was late, the full horror of the spectacle was revealed. One proprietor was so distressed when he saw the condition of his "cattle" that he auctioned them on the spot. It is recorded that only two years previously Lord Stafford had owned one of these unfortunate horses. It had cost him 150 guineas, but it had proved too much for him to handle and it had been sold to learn some discipline "on the road". It now fetched a sovereign, such was its condition. On another occasion one grossly overloaded coach was put on the weighbridge. To the amazement of all, it totalled four and a half tons, with the guard contributing some twenty stones.

The last day of the month was the hardest work for the horses as the coaches were laden with periodicals. It was known to all as magazine night. Many horses died in harness from overwork, and in the summer of 1821 it was recorded that some eighteen died on the long stages of the Great North Road.

Some of the best cared for horses on the road were the "Parliamentary" horses of the latter part of the era. Among a mass of legislation for the protection of the public was one stating that at no time must all four horses gallop together. This meant that the only way the mails could keep to time was by buying a fast trotter to put in every team so that it would trot while the other three horses galloped. As these horses were in great demand they were expensive to purchase and therefore everything was done for their wellbeing.

Most horses on the road were docked. This meant that a portion of the tail was amputated with a docking knife. The bleeding was then stopped with a hot iron. One of the worst side effects of this operation was blood poisoning which often followed if insufficient care was exercised.

The idea of this unpleasant operation was, in purely practical terms, sensible. Its purpose was to stop one of the leaders from swishing his tail over the rein. If this happened then the horse would often clamp his tail down firmly on the rein thus making control difficult. This practice was forbidden in most countries but it continued in England until the passing of the Docking and Nicking Act in 1949. The man responsible for pushing through the Bill was the late Sir Dymoke White Bt, a past president of the Coaching Club and an experienced and skilful whip.

Accidents

The fact that James Huskinson was run over and killed at the opening of the Liverpool and Manchester Railway gave great ammunition to the coach proprietors in their fight against the new and unwelcome invader. But coaching was dangerous and everyone knew it. The expression "to drop off" undoubtedly referred to those unfortunate travellers on a coach who did precisely that and broke their necks in a fall from the top of the moving vehicle. Many accidents were caused by rival coaches racing each other, such was the competition on important routes. Sometimes on the country routes standards were not as high and rotten harness or faulty equipment in inept hands was to blame.

The General Post Office and the large coach proprietors attempted to equate speed and safety by laying down regulations to be heeded by coachmen. Even so accidents happened and passengers were killed and injured. This early attempt to consolidate commonsense principles included warnings about driving furiously or drunkenly, obstructing the road and lighting lamps at dusk.

It had always been accepted that the coachman kept to the left of the highway. This custom dated back to early times when horsemen kept to the left to use their sword arms easily on encountering a hostile stranger. The coachman also found it kept his right hand free to use the whip while his left hand held the reins. Many coachmen thought that "rules were only for fools" and realised the folly of their ways only when an accident almost inevitably happened. An incident tarnished a coachman's image and he became viewed as expensive by his employers as he could lose them money and, perhaps more important, prestige.

"Rules were for fools"

Racing was a peril most passengers had to endure on the main highways. One of the most famous recorded rivalries on the road was between Captain Baring driving the Birmingham Tally-Ho and Captain Douglas of the Derby Mail. From this rivalry sprang the expression "a local derby". Needless to say this feud resulted in a serious accident when the mail ran into the Tally-Ho.

A delay for the Holyhead and Chester mails at Hockley Hill near Dunstable.
By courtesy of the Post Office

Sir St Vincent Cotton was responsible for what was possibly the most talked about accident of coaching days. This dashing young blood was at the reins of the Cambridge Star, having bribed the coachman to allow him to indulge his passion for driving. His enthusiasm, however, was too much and he overturned the coach while galloping on a stretch of the road. Mercifully everyone escaped with minor injuries except for an unfortunate Mr Calloway who broke a leg. This man, the champion jockey, was on his way to the races at Newmarket, and he was awarded £2 000 compensation against Robert Nelson and his partners who were the proprietors.

Another serious accident befell the London and Dorking coach. It left the Elephant and Castle with a full complement of passengers and arrived at Ewell where it stopped to deliver a parcel. The coach was driven by Joseph Walker who was also the proprietor, and, in common with many less fashionable coaches, it did not carry a guard. This meant that Walker had to get down from the box seat to go to the hind boot. Foolishly he left the reins in the hands of a boy who aspired to copy his hero of the box. He cracked the whip by mistake- the team took off at speed, the coach overturned and all the passengers were spilled off the roof seats. All were seriously hurt. One, a woman, fell on spiked railings and a contemporary account relates that "she lingered until the following day when she expired in the greatest agony".

The safety and stability of the coach rested to a great extent with the guard who was supposed to ensure that the luggage was evenly distributed on the vehicle's roof. If it was not loaded correctly it could make the coach rock violently and put everyone at great risk. If there was not a guard the responsibility was with the coachman who often did not have the time or inclination to see the job done properly. In 1811 a law was passed limiting the height to which luggage could be piled to two feet. The penalty for infringement was £5 for every extra inch above the maximum.

Smash in Piccadilly.
Author's collection

Patent safety coaches were soon to be seen of which the first was the Sovereign on the Brighton road. To reduce the centre of gravity no luggage or passengers were allowed on the roof. This coach was soon followed by Patent Safety and Life Preserver versions, but they were slower than the traditional coaches which continued to dominate the roads.

Storm, tempest, fog and floods accounted for many disasters and accidents. In the early 1800s, a winter of extreme severity saw more than thirty bridges washed away by rivers in spate, causing havoc with the coach schedules. Mail guards were fearful of the coming of winter as it was their responsibility to get the mail through in spite of the conditions. Many stories of heroism are recorded by these gallant men who sometimes sacrificed their lives in an attempt to reach the next town. In fog, men with creosote flares walked in front of the mails for their journeys out of London. Fog never stopped them running, whereas in deep snow all journeys were cancelled.

Soft snow was a danger as it collected in hard balls on the horses' feet, making it impossible for the animals to gain a secure foothold. To help overcome this hazard, tallow was put onto the sole of the foot. Ice was even more of a danger and horses were often shod with long frost nails to ensure they could keep their feet. The iron wheels compacted the ice and quickly made the coach into a lethal weapon, sliding sideways downhill taking horses and passengers with it in its mad slide.

The maxim followed by the nervous or timid traveller was "take the slow coach" which had its own band of devoted supporters who would rather die than travel on the fast and furious crack coaches. The press often over-sensationalised the accidents that were bound to happen to the 3 300 stage coaches and 700 mails which were on the road in 1837. Add a full complement of passengers and the 30 000 workers required to keep the coaches running and one may be forced to the conclusion that it was probably as safe as travelling on our crowded roads today.

JUST  ARRIVED,

And to be SEEN in a COMMODIOUS BOOTH,

During the Fair,

BALLARD's

GRAND COLLECTION OF

Wild Beasts,

Among which are, THE NOBLE

LIONESS,

FROM AFRICA,

Which attacked the Horse

In the Mail Coach, at Wintersloo Hut, near Salisbury, in October last, 1817
But was diverted from its Prey, by a large

MASTIFF DOG.

These Three Animals may now be seen together,
IN PERFECT AMITY !

For this unprecedented Accident, the Proprietor paid Mr. WEEKS the Value of the Horse; and Surveyors also were appointed to examine his Carriages, who pronounced them perfectly secure; nor would it ever been possible for the Animal to have broken out, but by the daring Attempt of some Person to plunder, who thereby loosened the Den.

THE ROYAL

Bengal Tiger

An Animal next in size and strength to the Lion, with whom it frequently contends, and the most savage and blood-thirsty of the brute Creation. When grown to maturity, it is able to run at full speed with a Buffalo or Horse on its back; and so daring, that it will attack, when hungry, the Camp itself. It was one of these Animals that seized the unfortunate Captain MUNRO, and bore him away in his Mouth, in the Face of his Companions, whilst out with a shooting Party, a few Years ago, in the Neighbourhood of Bengal.

THE REAL SENEGAL

LEOPARD,

The Beauty of which surpasses all Description.—The

Laughing Hyæna,

The same Kind of Animal that is described by BRUCE, in his Travels through the Deserts of Abyssinia, and are said to be so Untameable, that they dwell in Caves, and Caverns of the Earth, and so Blood-thirsty that they frequently take up the Bodies of the Dead; but this will prove the contrary of such Representation, it being perfectly Tame.

Also one of these scarce Animals, the

PORCUPINE,

A Native of the Interior of Africa, but now so extremely Rare, that it is even there seldom to be met with, and is the ONLY REAL PORCUPINE that has been exhibited for nearly Twenty Years. It has variegated Quills on its Back, 15 Inches long, and when provoked or attacked, it erects them so formidable in its Defence, as to form a complete Bulwark against all its Enemies, so that Nothing can injure them, as every Quill forms a Spear to its Pursuers, which are as Sharp as the Point of a Needle.—THE

OURANG OUTANG,

One of the most beautiful in Symmetry, and placid in temper ever yet exhibited. It stands Six Feet high, and its Limbs are astonishingly powerful. This Animal does any thing but speak.

The Black Bear,

OR POLAR MONSTER, JUST IMPORTED.
THE

Coatimondi, or Ant Eater,

From EGYPT, a very curious and interesting Animal, with a remarkable long Nose:

The JACKALL, or Lion's Provider;

This curious Animal provides Food for the Lion.

ALSO ONE OF THOSE SCARCE ANIMALS, CALLED THE

NEGRO FOLLOWERS,

FROM THE INTERIOR OF AFRICA.

It is customary for those Creatures to go in Droves, where they have an Opportunity to plunder the Natives of their Food,

THE INDIAN APE,

Who lost his Arm in an Engagement at Sea, in a British Ship,

With a Variety of other curious Animals, too numerous to insert.

Admittance, Ladies and Gentlemen, 1s.   Children and others, 6d.

BILLS of the largest Description, at an HOUR's Notice, by W. GLINDON, 48, Rupert Street, Haymarket, London.

Quicksilver and the Exeter Mail

The Quicksilver Devonport Mail was a legend. It was the only mail coach carrying a name, and its name imparted the essence of its fame—speed. It maintained ten and a quarter miles an hour between London and Devonport, including stops, and it was the fastest long distance mail in the country.

Romance and adventure surrounded the name of Quicksilver, and this was heightened by its route which included passing across Salisbury Plain and by Stonehenge in the early hours of the morning, a road it shared with the Exeter Mail made famous by one incident in particular, the attack by the lioness.

The attack near Salisbury

On October 20 1816 the coach was some few miles out of Salisbury. The coachman had been worried by the presence of what he assumed to be a large calf trotting beside the horses in the dark. He was unable positively to identify the beast and became further concerned by the behaviour of his team which could hardly be kept under control. On reaching Winterslow Hut, he stopped at the remote inn and immediately one of the leaders was attacked by the animal. The guard seized his blunderbuss and was on the point of shooting when some men ran up with a mastiff. They were in pursuit of a lioness which had escaped from a travelling menagerie. They immediately set the dog into the fray as a decoy. The lioness left the horse and seized the dog and tore it to pieces before she was captured by her keepers.

The lead horse, Pomegranate, was terribly injured but survived to be an exhibit in the travelling menagerie whose lioness had done the damage. After making a lot of money for the owners he was sold to work on the Brighton and Petworth Road where he worked for many years.

By courtesy of the Post Office

Another incident involved the down Quicksilver on a snowy night when the team were "springing the hill" outside Andover. The off-wheeler was run through by the shaft of a waggon coming, out of control, down Abbotts Hill. The horse was killed instantly and the coachman and guard were thrown from the coach. They picked themselves up, reunited themselves with their horses and continued on their way with three horses driven unicorn, and they arrived at Salisbury only forty-five minutes late after changing at the Pheasant, Winterslow Hut. The unicorn formation was used when one horse became lame on a stage and could not continue, and consisted of the two wheelers and one leader.

Another distinction of Quicksilver was that it left from the Gloucester Coffee House, Piccadilly, at 8 30 instead of from the General Post Office. This departure was shared with the other six West of England mails and was possibly to ease the congestion that no doubt was considerable with the other mails leaving St Martins-Le-Grand in quick succession. The mail was conveyed by mail cart to Piccadilly and the passengers by omnibus, therefore making the West Country mails rather special in the eyes of the public.

Quicksilver passes the Star & Garter, Kew Bridge, 1835.
By courtesy of the Post Office

Passengers alight from Quicksilver on a summer's day.

Quicksilver in particular became an untiring favourite with contemporary painters, including Pollard and Newhouse, and Sauerweid is well known for his portrayal of the lioness attacking the Exeter Mail.

With the opening of the London and Southampton railway, which reached Woking in May 1838 and Winchfield in September of the following year, Quicksilver's wings were clipped. *The Times* of October 1838 records: "About forty superior, good-sized, strengthy, short-legged, quick-actioned, fresh horses, and six sets of four-horse harness, which have been working the Exeter Telegraph, Southampton and Gosport fast coaches, and one stage of the Devonport Mail. The above genuine stock merits the particular attention of all persons requiring known good horses, which are for unreserved sale, entirely on account of the coaches being removed from the road to the railway."

The writing was on the wall for Quicksilver and all the crack coaches. The local Derby and Manchester Mail was one of the last to go—in October 1858. In the more remote parts of Scotland the era lingered on because of the nature of the country with its wild contours hindering the path of the railways. The fateful day was August 1 1874 when the Highland Railway opened and the last true mail coach started out on its final journey between Wick and Thurso.

One of the original Devonport mail coaches has survived. It was bought by Colonel J B Stracey-Clitherow who was a prominent coachman of the revival and after his retirement from the road he loaned it to the Museum of Transport, Hull. It stood idle until 1976 when it was reclaimed by the family and it is now in one of the coach houses at Hotham Hall, Humberside, a proud reminder of past glories.

45

Coaching characters

The stage waggon drivers of the era that preceded the Golden Age of Coaching were a true reflection of the roads they travelled and the hardships they endured. They wore many layers of mud-encrusted clothes and were a rough and tough breed of men who were generally figures of fun. They were in basic terms drovers of animals in sharp contrast to the highly skilled and heroic coachmen who were soon to make such an impact on the history of transportation. This new breed were artists in handling their reins and in the management of their horses on all roads in all weathers. Beautifully turned out, confident and authoritative, they were the symbol of all that coaching had achieved.

The accepted dress for a coachman on one of the crack roads was a well cut and stylish box-cloth coat surmounted by a beaver hat and a dashing spotted cravat. The real extroverts in dress and mannerisms were known as flashmen and were the flamboyant characters of the road. Men such as Sam Haywood, who drove the Wonder between the Hen & Chickens, Birmingham, and the Lion, Shrewsbury. He was a skilled whip and was famed for the feat he performed nightly after crossing the English Bridge. He then galloped up Wyle Cop and drove in through the inn archway at a smart trot, reminding his outside passengers to mind their heads. The whole manoeuvre was timed to a nicety and the coach had only inches to spare on each side. Passengers who had not experienced that feat were most alarmed but the townspeople loved to watch the spectacle of the coach arriving.

Deeds of skill and daring were well recorded and they were the talk of princes and paupers who avidly followed their exploits. Above all, they were supremely confident of their art, and this gave them the ability to converse with all classes and to drive difficult teams in every weather.

Only the most determined and promising rose to drive four horses, and when the pinnacle of success had been achieved it was hard and demanding work. A coachman had to augment his salary by accepting or shouldering passengers without the proprietor's knowledge or allowing some wealthy young man to take the reins. This last act was rightly considered a very serious offence as it was the cause of many accidents and was punishable by instant dismissal and a fine of between £5 and £10 at the discretion of the magistrates.

Many young men of noble birth turned to the box seat after squandering a fortune at the gaming tables. It was the one profession that could still offer a gentleman in reduced circumstances nation-wide renown. Prominent among these were Sir St Vincent Cotton who for many years drove the Age on the Brighton road. Educated at Westminster and Christ Church, Oxford, he was known to the other more humble professionals on the Brighton road as the Baronet. He was rewarded for his skill on the box by an income of some £300 a year, but this did little to comfort him for the loss of his previous income of £5 000 a year. Others included Harry Stevenson, known on the road as the Cambridge graduate. Nimrod says of him that he was a supreme artist "whose passion for the bench exceeded all other worldly ambitions". We are also reminded that he always remembered the social graces of his birth and was "singularly refined and courteous".

The coachman enjoyed the deference shown to him on the road. He was almost always cheerful, helpful to young travellers and keen to impress his passengers with the quality of his team and the speed and regularity of the coach. In the

Among the great coachmen

46

Sir St Vincent Cotton, the baronet who took to the Road professionally.

inn yard, he was the man all the urchins looked up to, and every scruffy youth would ape his lordly gait. They all longed to mount his "throne" and in their dreams they drove many a mile behind his straining steeds. Most were doomed to the humble life of an ostler, looking after the horses and changing teams in under fifty seconds for the demanding coachman. Life on the road was hard, and there were many disappointments for those who chose to make it their life.

Some of the more enlightened proprietors provided subsidised meals for their coachmen and guards and perhaps the most famous was Mrs Nelson of the Bull Inn in Whitechapel. Here the company dined with considerable ceremony and entertained the occasional amateur coachman like Thomas Kenyon and Sir Henry Peyton. Even Charles Dickens accepted an invitation to dine in this sanctum, and no doubt listened enthralled to the tales of the week's incidents. Mrs Nelson's son Robert, who drove the Exeter Defiance, presided over the assembled company when he was in London. On other occasions his place was taken by the oldest coachman who would propose the loyal toast in the appropriate manner. A guard was never allowed to preside or usurp the coachman's privileges. Each coachman and guard in this room was referred to by the name of his road, giving the conversation a strange formal ring. In this company the crude drovers of the early stage waggons would have looked very out of place. The march of progress had been swift.

Coaching customs and conduct

It was often said that the real test of a gentleman was his behaviour when a coach stopped en route for the refreshment of its weary passengers. The journey often turned them into starving savages who would descend on the dining room, demanding service. The true gentleman would escort a lady from the coach, ensure she was provided with dinner and pay her bill. This inevitably meant that it was impossible for him to eat himself as time was strictly limited. The inn-keepers would often exacerbate the situation by delaying the food so passengers had little time to eat their fill before they had to be on the road again.

Many of the better-run inns supplied local delicacies which achieved a wide fame. Friends and relations would often ask the traveller to purchase them at the inns where the coach parties stopped for refreshment, and prominent among these was the Bell Inn, at Stilton, on the Great North Road between Huntingdon and Stamford. It saw an endless procession of coaches and carriages, many of which stopped to change horses and refresh weary passengers.

It was regrettable that none of the cheeses sold at the Bell was ever made at Stilton but imported from Wymondham in Leicestershire. The list of other famed delicacies is endless—York Hams, Banbury Cakes, Bath Buns, Everton Toffee and Shrewsbury Cakes.

The coaching inns were open twenty-four hours a day and provided a multitude of services. Not only did they provide rest and refreshment for the passengers who arrived by coach but they also looked after the stabling and welfare of the horses.

The head yard porter was in charge of the stables and ran his yard as a benevolent dictator. To him came the young bloods anxious for a place on the box seat next to the coachman which would be arranged for a fee. In busy yards he would command a weekly income from tips of around £5 and it was important for the regular traveller to be on the right side of him if favours were required. He, in turn, was answerable to the proprietor if the horses and harness were not turned out to perfection.

Before the average citizen set out to travel by stage coach he would take care to survey the market carefully and weigh up the rival coaches thrusting for his business. Once he had made up his mind, he would go to the booking office where the clerk would enter his name in the ledger and issue a ticket for the journey. Great care was taken to avoid overbooking as the cost of conveying any passenger in this unfortunate circumstance was charged to the clerk responsible. This could prove expensive as the extra customer would usually be sent by post-chaise at a cost of up to one shilling a mile unless he was forgiving enough to wait for the next coach.

The journey itself could be the cause of abject misery or sheer elation for the passenger. The weather could be foul and the company uncongenial. On the contrary, it could be an experience to savour on a fine summer morning with lively and interesting fellow travellers to converse with in the fresh country air. Contemporary cartoonists lampooned the stage coach passenger who was forced to spend many hours inside the coach with a fat woman carrying a parrot and a fishmonger smelling of his wares.

Travellers' joys and woes

48

The Bell Inn at Stilton in its heyday, painted by Luke Sykes.

The proprietor of the Castle Hotel, Brighton, once wrote that "a woman was a creature to be looked at, admired, courted, and beloved in a stage coach". No doubt he knew what he was talking about, and would have approved of the initiative of a young man travelling on the Glasgow and Edinburgh coach.

When the young lady of his affections had booked her seat, he quickly booked all the other inside seats. He was amply rewarded for his enterprise: before the journey's end the lady agreed to marry him. But sadly this romantic start to their relationship was not to continue after marriage. Such diversions on the road were however the exception rather than the rule.

On a well appointed coach like the Beehive, travellers were provided with reading lamps. No doubt the cramped passengers, who paid dearly for their inside seats in the depth of a hard winter, tired of reading and looked for other ways of whiling the time away. Cards were an obvious choice but for the seasoned traveller the firm favourite was the road game or road piquette as it was sometimes called.

The idea of the game was that each group would choose one side of the road and look for certain objects or animals which were given specific values. Reynardson, in Down the Road, tells us that "A donkey counted seven, a pig one, a black sheep one, a cat five, a cat in a window ten, a dog one, a magpie one, a grey horse five; and there was one thing by which game might be got at once, but it was connected by what I cannot venture to describe, and it was a very rare occurrence. Once in my life, and only once, I saw this feat performed, and it elicited a shout of 'Game, by Jove!'."

Time-bill of the Wonder coach from London to Shrewsbury:

Proprietor	Place	Miles	Time Allowed		Should Arrive
Despatched from Bull and Mouth at 6.30 morning					
" " Peacock, Islington, at 6.45 o'clock					
			H.	M.	
Sherman . . .	St. Albans . .	22½	2	3	8.48
J. Liley . . .	Redbourn . .	4½	0	25	9.13
	(Breakfast) .	—	0	20	—
Goodyear . . .	Dunstable . .	8¼	0	48	10.21
Sheppard . . .	Daventry . .	29¾	2	54	2.15
Collier	Coventry . .	19	1	47	4.2
	(Business) . .	—	0	5	—
Vyse	Birmingham . .	19	1	39	5.46
	(Dinner) . .	—	0	35	—
Evans	Wolverhampton	14	1	15	7.36
	(Business) . .	—	0	5	—
	Summerhouse .	6½	0	35	8.16
J. Taylor . . .	Shifnal . . .	6½	0	35	8.51
H. J. Taylor . .	Haygate . . .	8	0	43	9.34
J. Taylor . . .	Shrewsbury . .	10	0	56	10.30
		158	15	45	

Time-bill of the Manchester Telegraph:

Proprietor	Place	Miles	Time Allowed		Should Arrive
Leave Bull and Mouth at 5 a.m.					
" Peacock, Islington, at 5.15					
			H.	M.	
Sherman . . .	St. Albans . .	19½	1	54	7.9
Liley	Redbourn . .	4½	0	22	7.31
Fossey	Hockliffe . .	12½	1	10	8.41
	Northampton .				
	(Breakfast) .	—	0	20	—
Shaw	Harboro' . .	47½	4	30	1.31
	Leicester . . .				
	(Business) . .	—	0	5	—
Pettifer . . .	Loughboro' . .	26	2	27	4.3
	Derby . . .				
	(Dinner) . .	—	0	20	—
Mason	Ashbourne . .	30	2	48	7.11
Wood	Waterhouses .	7½	0	43	7.54
Linley	Bullock Smithy .	29½	2	36	10.40
Wetherall & Co .	Manchester . .	9	0	50	11.30
		186	18	15	

The Golden Age

The rivals of the road

Palmer's mail coach revolution had sparked off fierce competition between the stage coaches whose proprietors were anxious to get a share of the ever-increasing number of people travelling on business or pleasure. The mail coaches were on specific contract from the Post Office and carried both mail and a strictly limited number of passengers. The stage coaches carried most of the passengers, travelling the length and breadth of the country, and they were backed by large organisations presided over by such giants as Chaplin, Horne and Sherman.

It was Sherman who established in 1825 the famous Shrewsbury Wonder which ran from the Bull & Mouth, London, to the Lion Hotel, Shrewsbury, in his well known black and yellow livery. This became a very profitable service and was characterised by speed and, above all, punctuality. Many proprietors cast envious eyes on the revenues derived from the road, and in 1834 a consortium headed by Horne set up an opposition coach called the Nimrod. Sherman was in no mood to surrender his pre-eminence on this route and, in fighting mood, he put the Stag on the road the next season. It was timed to run in advance of the Nimrod while the Wonder followed some little time later. This clever move ensured that the Nimrod was effectively sandwiched and was more often than not poorly patronised.

The coaches maintained a mad pace, and on one dread day the coachman of the Nimrod was thrown off and killed on the Wolverhampton to Shrewsbury stage. The Wonder had previously been renowned for its speed of eleven and a half miles per hour, but now caution was thrown to the winds, and often all three coaches would arrive up to two hours in advance of their published arrival times.

While fighting off the challenge of the Nimrod, Sherman reduced his fares on the Wonder and Stag by one-third, and in one year he and his partners lost a reputed £1 500. This eventually resulted in the Nimrod being withdrawn and fares were raised to their previous level.

There was also keen rivalry on the road to Manchester, known to travellers from London as Cottonopolis. The demands of trade ensured there was plenty of business for stage coaches such as the Manchester Defiance which was started in 1821. Its speed failed to live up to its provocative name as it took twenty-seven hours from London, averaging six miles an hour, which was reduced to twenty-four hours the next year. It was renamed Royal Defiance in 1826 but it still took twenty-four hours.

Sherman gained control of the old Manchester Telegraph which had previously limped home in twenty-nine and a half hours. He ran it from the Bull & Mouth at 5 am and it arrived in Manchester at 11 30 pm the same day. Chaplin was not prepared to stand idly by so he took over the Defiance and matched the Telegraph for speed. Sherman countered and reduced the time taken by the Telegraph to cover the one hundred and eighty-six miles from London to Manchester by one hour, averaging twelve miles per hour, including a stop for twenty minutes at Derby for lunch and time for changing horses en route.

Competing with these fast coaches came the Peveril of the Peak and the Red Rover. The latter was chiefly noted for the red harness and collars the horses sported and for the red hats of the guards which were not totally approved of and certainly not considered in the best tradition of the road.

The Opposition Coaches: a famous aquatint engraved and painted by Charles Cooper Henderson.

The Beehive was the venture of Robert Nelson who had been dispossessed of the Red Rover by Sherman and was determined to establish himself on the Manchester road. It was the pullman of its era and was fitted with reading lamps for the passengers and with spring cushions. It left La Belle Sauvage, Ludgate Hill, at 8 every morning and arrived in Manchester the following morning in time for passengers to join the Scottish coaches.

Another departure from normal practice was the introduction of a coach card which specified the seat the passenger had booked. This eliminated distasteful wrangles over where passengers should sit, which often resulted in the losers being in sullen mood for the journey.

Any parcel sent on the Beehive was guaranteed to be delivered to the outskirts of London within two hours of the arrival of the coach—a remarkable achievement by any standards.

He further endeared himself to his passengers by forbidding the carrying of fish!

The smaller proprietors who served suburban London at this time built up a good trade conveying passengers who had just arrived in the capital and those who wished to join the long-distance coaches leaving for the provinces. They operated within a radius of some twenty miles of the city and were usually pair-horse vehicles making up to two journeys a day.

Shillibeer introduced his omnibus in 1829 which did much to increase the comfort of his passengers. He had served in the Royal Navy, and he manned the service with some of his former shipmates. When professional coachmen had to be employed it was the beginning of the end for Shillibeer who was at the mercy of dishonest drivers who misappropriated the fares. He was forced to let other contractors take over the business after some six years and eventually set up as an undertaker.

Needless to say these pair-horse omnibuses were despised by long distance four-horse coachmen who regarded themselves as the uncrowned kings of the road.

The Golden Age, which is generally accepted as spanning the era from 1824 to 1848, set new standards of speed and efficiency, and the roads of Britain were the envy of the world. Coaching had reached a zenith which no system of transport has ever equalled. It was, needless to say, a paradise for the sportsman who revelled in the finely matched teams of horses and smart coaches to be seen on every road in the kingdom. But competition was however fierce among the proprietors and only the best organised survived.

Change and decay

When Stephenson's Locomotion Number One had clattered through from Stockton to Darlington in 1825, few people believed it could rival the supremacy of the horse except in the carriage of heavy goods. But over the next decade railways changed from a dangerous fantasy into a viable and far faster means of travel. The travel industry was entering a period of rapid technological development and there was nothing remotely technological or ingenious about a coach and four any more.

The world of coaching shivered and caught its first serious cold when William Chaplin sold his interest in the road and switched his allegiance to the railways. Not all the proprietors were so far sighted, and Sherman showed a reckless disdain for the facts by attempting to join battle with the steaming "tea kettles" as they were known. His misplaced faith cost him some £7 000. Coaching was in its death throes and as the national mode of transport. The Great Western Railway even adopted a wide gauge so it could carry coaches—such was the final ignominy.

Nothing is more surprising about the story of coaching than the fact that it ended so quickly.

The coachmen on the Great North Road would point to the earthworks of the London and Birmingham railway with lofty disdain. They felt that the hundreds of sweating navvies moving mountains of earth were on a fools errand, and their passengers agreed with them.

In 1838 the London and Birmingham railway opened and the number of coaches leaving Birmingham for London dwindled in that year from twenty-two to four. Those shrewd investors who had risked so much in the gamble on the railways were now set to gather a rich harvest.

On May 11 1840 the last coach deserted the run from London to York. The Great North Road began to decline in earnest, and its final death knell sounded when the Edinburgh mail was discontinued in 1842.

Many of the displaced coachmen and guards found employment with the railway companies. Others became innkeepers on the road they had travelled so regularly in the past, but this was not in general a lucrative occupation as, when the stage coaches went off the road, the inns suffered a disastrous loss of trade. Some entered into employment in private stables with wealthy patrons who had long admired their skill on the box, but they were the fortunate minority.

Just a few years previously there had been more than 3 000 coachmen secure in their jobs. They now were humbled from their privileged box, and those who were lucky found employment as omnibus drivers.

The railways were to capitalize on speed as the mail and stage coaches had done. In an effort to frighten potential train passengers, the coach proprietors offered to build cemeteries outside the railway stations as they claimed there would be great loss of life. But nothing was to stop the growth of the railways, and within a hundred years the network covered nearly every village and town in Britain.

At that point the wheel really had come full circle for the railways suffered a huge slump in business and Dr Beeching's axe was soon to fall with severity.

When the "tea kettle" came

The Louth-London mail coach leaves on its last journey from Louth on 19 December 1845—by rail, on the newly opened Peterborough-Blisworth line.
By courtesy of the Post Office

The explosion in private motoring in the 1950s ensured that the roads had regained their place as the country's major transport artery.

But what had happened to the pioneer spirit that foresaw the possibility of journeying across country when the romance of travel was there for all to savour and every journey was an adventure?

We now pay our own small tribute to the swell dragsman and his fiery team as the ghosts come back to watch fearfully as the evil smelling, noisy motor car enslaves us.

Highway robbery

The profession followed by Duval, Turpin and other notorious figures was not lacking in eager recruits. In fact the roads of Britain positively bustled with their activity and they kept passengers on the highway in a permanent state of apprehension. Rarely were the highwaymen the glamorous figures they have been made out to be, and they were often cheap thieves with no scruples. England was the only country in Europe which was unable to boast a full-time paid police force, so very few were caught.

Claude Duval was born in 1643, the son of a miller in Normandy. It is thought that he gained employment with English Royalist exiles he had met in Paris and came to England when Charles II came to the throne. He drifted out of a safe way of life as a servant and we first hear of him in 1668 when £10 was offered for his capture.

The best known story of Duval's career was that of the celebrated hold-up on Hounslow Heath when he asked the lady passenger to alight and dance the coranto. The dance over, he escorted her to her coach and asked her husband to hand over his money. Duval well knew that he was carrying £400, but he was satisfied when he was handed a bag containing £100 and with good grace remarked "This liberality of yours shall excuse you the other £300".

His final capture was something of an anti-climax as he was arrested drunk in a London inn. He was tried and in January 1670, at the age of 27, he was hanged at Tyburn. He was accompanied to the gallows by his lady admirers who then had his body taken to the Tangier Tavern, St Giles's. His mourners came to a macabre room draped in black attended by eight men in black cloaks and masks. After his funeral he was buried at St Paul's Church, Covent Garden.

In contrast to the impeccable manners of Duval, Turpin was a rough and brutish man. He was born in 1705 at the Crown Inn, Hempstead, Essex. After serving his apprenticeship as a butcher, he set up his own shop at the age of 21 in Waltham Abbey, but his sheep stealing to stock his shop soon made him flee the town.

Pretending to be a revenue officer, he held up smugglers until they became suspicious and again he fled, this time to join the infamous Gregory's Gang. He was involved in a series of robberies noted for their violence and senseless cruelty, and soon there was a reward of £50 offered for the capture of any of the notorious group. This was raised to £100 and five of the gang were captured. Turpin escaped by jumping out of a window.

Then, at the age of 30, he began his life on the highway, and he was soon the most feared highwayman in England. He teamed up with Tom King in 1737 to terrorise and rob travellers around Epping Forest. They worked untiringly in pursuit of a rich harvest. The partnership was dissolved when Turpin shot King by mistake when a constable challenged him over a stolen grey colt called Whitestockings. Turpin returned to his trade and continued robbing coaches and travellers until an amazing additional reward of £200 was offered for his arrest.

Life became too dangerous for him from the reward seekers and he retired to Yorkshire where he was eventually arrested and convicted. He was hanged on April 7 1739 at the age of 34. He died the most infamous of all the highwaymen

Adventure on the road

By courtesy of the Post Office

Claud Duval dancing on Hounslow Heath.
Radio Times Hulton Picture Library

Dick Turpin clearing the Old Hornsey toll bar gate to the surprise of his pursuers.
Radio Times Hulton Picture Library

with the legend of Black Bess as his public memorial. It is doubtful whether this black mare ever existed, and Harrison Ainsworth's picture of the romantic hero Turpin is far from the truth.

Many of the landlords of the inns on the main roads were in league with the highwaymen. They were well placed to pass on information about the movements of those who stayed at their establishments. Armed with this knowledge, it was easy for the highwaymen to relieve rich and genteel travellers of their possessions.

Nervous travellers were made even more apprehensive as they saw corpses of highwaymen swinging from gibbets by the side of the road. Those who were hanged were often accompanied on their last journey to the gallows by chaplains or ordinaries, a bunch of charlatans and debauchees who made a living by selling the last words of the convicted to the local press—the few the law had caught up with, but they were the unlucky ones, and the majority roamed freely to pursue their profession.

Coaching painters

Not until coaching was revered and romanticised did it attract the eyes and brush of the artist. It was also soon to be regarded as a sport which made it a much more commercial subject for the etcher. Etching in aquatint was introduced into Britain about 1775 and a coaching scene was a splendid way of demonstrating the delicate tints and colours of this new medium.

James Pollard is possibly the best known of artists who specialised in coaching pictures. His father was an engraver and publisher, and he was born in Spa Fields, London, in 1791. Most of his pictures were engraved and it is said, perhaps unkindly, that they gained in this process in the hands of capable craftsmen. He is buried in Hornsey churchyard not far from the great coaching road out of London along which he must have seen the subjects of his pictures passing so often when he was a young man.

Perhaps the best known after Pollard is Approach to Christmas. This splendid scene has all the classic ingredients of Christmas cards. Another Pollard aquatint, A North-East View of the General Post Office, was published in 1832. This represented one of the sights of London with the mail coaches gathering before their departure to all parts of the country.

His contemporary, Henry Alken, was born in Suffolk but spent much of his life in London. His output was prodigious and his pictures also benefited from his first-hand knowledge of horses as he was a great sportsman.

Often he engraved his own pictures, and was known to have been engraver to other painters. He was in demand by publishers to illustrate sporting books, and, above all, his prints sold to a ready market. His son, also named Henry, was also a keen follower of the road, but he was capable of producing only a fair imitation of his father's work. This enabled him, however, to take full advantage of the signature "H Alken" when selling his work.

Another artist with a close personal love for his subject was Charles Cooper Henderson, the son of well-to-do parents who hoped he would be called to the bar. His father disinherited him when he turned his back on the profession he had chosen for his son, and Charles turned to painting in both oils and water colour. He somehow had a magical touch which captured not only the speed and movement of the coach and horses but also the spirit of the age.

Rudolph Ackermann published two aquatints engraved by J Harris depicting the Taglioni Windsor coach, and soon after Fores published a series based on Henderson's work. A second important series produced by Fores was called Coaching Incidents which was outstandingly successful. But by 1850 his output virtually ceased as he was left a fortune by his mother which removed the creative urge, and he went into retirement near Chertsey.

From 1830 to 1845 Charles B Newhouse was at work in water colours. He produced some vignetted sketches which R G Reeve aquatinted and these were published in 1833. He concentrated mainly on depicting northern roads but he is also well known for his view of Temple Bar by moonlight showing the Quicksilver arriving. Speed was his god, and his pictures are full of motion showing crack teams of blood horses usually moving at a great pace.

W J Shayer delighted in painting coaches travelling on the roads of southern

Charles Cooper Henderson's painting, The Olden Time, probably depicts the Bull & Mouth Inn, London.
By courtesy of the Post Office

Approach to Christmas.

England. From his father, William Shayer, he inherited a love of rural and coastal scenes which he frequently used as backgrounds to his pictures. He was meticulous in his attention to detail and he faithfully portrayed the smallest details of harness and appointments.

Yet another amateur coachman to put brush to canvas was Lynwood Palmer. At his home he kept harness horses and indulged his passion for fast driving, usually when there was little traffic on the road in the evening. He had a splendid collection of sporting vehicles and a harness room that was beautifully maintained in the classic tradition. As a young man he had spent many years with horses in western America and Canada. In later years he was a leading authority on shoeing. He died in 1941, leaving a great legacy of pictures which faithfully captured the character of the subject he loved so much.

Our contemporary and faithful guard, Luke Sykes, lists among his talents an aptitude as a sporting artist. His picture of the Bell at Stilton (page 49) was commissioned especially for the film and certainly depicts the spirit of the road and all its associations. Because of his own involvement in coaching, small details of harness and correct appointments flow easily from his brush.

The coaching revival and James Selby

The Golden Age of Coaching was dead and the pavements of Piccadilly were bereft of the coaches carrying the public to all corners of the land. Only in country districts did public coaching survive, and this had little of the romance of the roads of yesterday.

But the memory lingered on in the hearts of many sporting amateurs who had been conveyed to their public schools by coach. In 1866 the slumber that coaching had suffered showed signs of an awakening. A band of enthusiasts lead by the Duke of Beaufort, Captain Haworth and Colonel Armitage joined together and put a coach on the road between London and Brighton on alternate days. Unfortunately it proved a failure and was discontinued after a season, but it did nothing to dampen the enthusiasm of devotees. In 1867 Mr Chandos Pole and friends put a coach on the Brighton road every day, and by 1873 there were some twelve coaches running out of London.

The coaches of this new era were known as road coaches and were turned out with great care. Their wealthy proprietors never expected receipts to match expenditure as they regarded the pleasures of coaching as their reward. They picked the best roads, employed the best coaching professionals and used the best horses.

James Selby, the most respected coachman of his era.

With this tide of interest in coaching, many private stables put teams on the road. The vehicles they used were similar in most respects to the road coaches and were called drags. They were however lighter and more refined and carried no lettering, only the discreet crest or monogram of the owner. Two liveried grooms were carried in place of the guard. They were the perfect vehicles with which the extrovert horseman could entertain his guests and show off a perfectly matched and mannered team of horses. But these private coaches never travelled the roads of Britain on regular runs and they possessed little of the romance of the road as their forebears had known it.

James Selby, however, was the one man who was able to rekindle the spark that set everyone talking about his coaching exploits. In 1870 we first hear of him driving the Tunbridge Wells coach, owned by Lord Bective, in the summer, and the St Albans coach in the winter. He then took the bold step of entering into partnership with Mr Cowland and they set up the coach-building firm of Cowland and Selby. Cowland had a wealth of experience with the famous makers Holland & Holland in London, and he was well qualified to build coaches of style and quality.

Selby asked his partner to build a light, handsome coach for him to use on the St Albans road and the service he established continued for eleven years. He was no fair-weather coachman and ran in all weathers, winter and summer. It is recorded that he left the White Horse Cellar in London in January 1881 in a severe snowstorm with Major Dixon ("Dickey the Driver"). On arrival, Selby was so cold that his hat could be removed only by pouring warm water into the brim as it was frozen to his head. Among the professionals, he was perhaps the best known and revered of coachmen driving out of London.

In 1879 he went to France at the invitation of Captain Cropper to help run a coach from Paris to Versailles. This caused a mild sensation as it was the first coach to be run in France on the lines of the English revival coaches.

Text labels within illustration:
THE VIVID
HAMPTON COURT

THE EXCELSIOR.
TUNBRIDGE WELLS.

ABERDEEN PLACE

MR SELBY'S SERVANTS

THE OLD T
VIRGIN

HALL ROAD N.W

This was how Illustrated Newspapers Limited recorded the funeral cortege of Selby on the road to Highgate Cemetery

62

THE WONDER.
ST ALBANS

THE DEFIANCE.
BENTLEY PRIORY

THE COMET
BRIGHTON

THE NEW TIMES.
GUILDFORD.

THE PERSEVERANCE.
DORKING

MAIDA
VALE
N.W

THE OLD TIMES.
(BRIGHTON).

J. Swain Eng.

in December 1888.

In 1888 he put his coach, Old Times, on the Brighton road in opposition to the Comet which was an established success on that famous run. The venture was financed by wealthy sporting figures who paid for the privilege of driving on certain prescribed days. The Old Times left from the White Horse Cellar in Piccadilly and ended its journeys at the Old Ship Hotel on Tuesdays, Thursdays and Saturdays. Journeys from Brighton were made on Mondays, Wednesdays and Fridays. Occasionally he would make the double journey in the day, and on one notable day he made the return journey of 108 miles within nine hours. This led to his feats being discussed by his supporters as Ascot, and ultimately resulted in a wager being made against the possibility of the return journey within eight hours. Selby accepted the challenge. He was to receive £1 000 if he was successful, and he was to forfeit £500 if he failed.

Preparations were made and the smallest details were attended to before the morning of July 13 1888 arrived when the attempt was to be made. Grooms were practised in changing horses as fast as possible and considerable rivalry sprang up among them. The horses were hard and fit, and everything was ready for the great challenge. The police were prepared to turn a blind eye to what could amount to a furious-driving charge and even helped to clear the traffic on the route.

A few minutes before 10 o'clock the Old Times arrived in front of the White Horse Cellar to be met by a throng of supporters and admirers. The privileged

The challenge for £1 000

Friendly rivalry on the road to the races.
Author's collection

''In Memoriam''

Air — ''Good Old Jeff''.
They say its just ten years ago since
  since Selby's coach first ran,
With good old Major Dixon on, a tho-
  rough coaching man.
The coach has never missed a day, no
  matter hail or snow,
Jim Selby's motto always was, the
  ''Old Times'' still must go.

Chorus.

We'll ne'er see more that dear old face,
  those eyes in death are dim;
He's done his stage and done it well,
  our friend and favourite Jim.

In January eighty-one the snow lay far
  and wide,
Still Selby struggled bravely on, the
  Major by his side;

The best of friends they were in life,
  now both are gone to rest.
It seems that those who leave us now
  are those we love the best.
The last ride that our old friend had
  was on the Brighton road,
Whilst he with favourite anecdote
  amused his sporting load;
But now he's left us all to mourn for
  him so kind and true,
Respected both by rich and poor — in
  fact, by all he knew.
Ne'er shall I ride another stage with
  him I loved so well,
Or tootle on his favourite horn the tunes
  to me he'd tell;
For now he's gone to realms above all
  pleasure here is marred:
A good old master and a friend was he
  to me, his Guard.

Walter Godden.

Miss A Sylvia Brocklebank driving her team of Hackneys.
Author's collection

The guard nearly gets left behind.
Author's collection

passengers were Messrs Beckett, Broadwood, Cosier, McAdam and Carlton Blyth, and the guard was Walter Godden (whom we are to meet later on Mr Vanderbilt's coach). On the stroke of ten they were off and made excellent progress out of London.

All went well on the down journey and two changes of horses were made in forty-seven seconds, so that when they arrived in Brighton they had covered the fifty-four miles from Piccadilly in three hours and fifty-six minutes. The coach stopped at the Old Ship for a matter of seconds and then was off again with its straining team to gallop its way back to London. Luck was with them and the coach left Purley Bottom at 4 52, well on schedule.

Selby and his friends sensed they were near to their goal and were in jubilant mood. "Bravo! Jim" yelled cabbies feverish with excitement as they galloped across Chelsea Bridge. Godden sounded his triumphant horn and the Old Times raced into Piccadilly to pull up at 5 50—with some ten minutes to spare!

Selby had become the sporting giant of the road. He had averaged 13·97 mph, using eight teams and making fourteen changes.

All this publicity ensured that the Old Times was well filled in summer, so Selby boldly decided to stay in business all winter. On December 7 he drove up from Brighton for the last time. He had contracted pneumonia and died suddenly at the age of 45, to the sorrow of all who knew him. At his funeral an enormous procession of carriages and coaches followed his coffin to Highgate Cemetery. To this day visitors may see his memorial in the private section of the cemetery.

The Old Times was sold at Aldridge's soon after his death and was used until 1914 by various proprietors including Lord Leconfield. For many years an Old Times dinner was held by Selby's friends at which Walter Godden would sound the coach horn and recite his own lines in praise of the great coachman.

On December 14 1938, the fiftieth anniversary of Selby's death, a plaque was unveiled in London on the site of Selby's former home in Edgware Road commemorating the great man. Mr Bernard Mills, the present owner of the Old Times, was driving the famous coach on that occasion, and his passengers were old coachmen, some of whom had known Selby and vividly recalled his great feats. The plaque was supposed lost in the blitz but was later recovered and now rests in the wall of Mr Mills' Gloucestershire coachhouse which houses the Old Times.

In the period between the two great wars coaching was continued on a smaller scale by a devoted band of enthusiasts who kept the old traditions alive. It was then a matter of doleful speculation as to whether the new world that emerged after 1945 would ever see coaching men again. Needless to say, the excitement and lure of the box seat soon had a respectable number of teams on the road.

Perhaps the greatest achievement of the post war years was the famous Tulip run between Istanbul and Rotterdam. This was a remarkable journey of some 2 175 miles which was completed in thirty-nine days by Mr Van de Touw.

The spirit of our coaching ancestors is alive and well, and the ghosts of the past must be well pleased with today's coaching activities.

2 175 miles completed in thirty-nine days

The Americans

The first American to succumb to the lure of the road in England was W G Tiffany. Such was his enthusiasm that he had two coaches built in London, the first by Peters in 1868 and the second by Laurie and Marner in 1873. In that year he put both coaches on the London to Brighton road after taking lessons from Charles Warde, one of the best known of the old mail coachmen. "Mr Tiffany did the thing very well" recalled a contemporary commentator.

While Tiffany was the first American to drive regularly in England, Colonel Delancey Kane came over two years later and enjoyed a season coaching before taking his yellow coach Tally-Ho to America. Once back home he put it on a modest fifteen-mile run from New York to Pelham.

On Venture to Brighton

No story of coaching in England is complete without the mention of Alfred Gwynne Vanderbilt, that remarkable capitalist and sportsman. He was a man of simple tastes despite his enormous wealth, but his one extravagance was his love of horses and coaching in particular. In 1907 he came to England with twenty-seven horses and a determination to show that he was the match for the best in England. He set up his stables at Red Hill Farm, north west of London, and to the amazement of the crowd won first time out at the International Horse Show.

Right
A G Vanderbilt at the Hotel Metropole, Brighton.
Author's collection

Left
Vanderbilt driving his famous team of greys to the Venture.
Author's collection

Not only were his horses and coach beautifully turned out, but the man himself drove with such style and elegance. Venture, Viking, Vanity and Vogue were the four horses that the crowd would not forget driven to the Venture coach by Vanderbilt! He longed to join the immortals on the famous Brighton and London road, and to this end he laid plans to come to Britain in the spring of 1908. He brought with him eighty horses bought in America from the Fiss Doerr and Carol Coach Horse Company. E Vow der Horst Koch was to be joint coachman, driving the Viking.

The Venture was put on the road in May 1908 with Walter Godden as guard. It left the Hotel Victoria at 11 o'clock precisely. The famous greys set off boldly on the first stage of their fifty-seven-mile journey to Brighton to a rendition of "The Bonnie, Bonnie Banks of Loch Lomond" played on the key bugle. The *Daily Express* recorded that "Crowds, many ranks deep, lined the way right through London. People rushed out of shops and joined the cries of 'Good Luck' and 'Good Old Vandy!'."

Mrs Reginald Vanderbilt was on the box seat, and all the passengers wore flowers of red and white—the Vanderbilt colours. The rain kept off for the run but a mist hung over the country denying Vanderbilt's guests on the coach the wonderful view from Reigate Hill. At 5 32 pm the coach pulled into the Hotel Metropole's portico while Walter Godden blew his new Venture call on the coach horn.

Vanderbilt was asked the inevitable question: What was the cost of this adventure? He replied that he did not wish to make it pay and he meant it. "Just sport" was his only aim and that is precisely what he had in abundance on this historic road. His outgoings were enormous, however, far outweighing the sum of £500 that he could collect from passengers over the seven weeks the service was to last. This was of course assuming that the coach was full, every trip, of passengers who paid for the privilege of riding.

The public loved this handsome figure who became the popular and romantic hero of the road, and in 1909, encouraged by public acclaim, he ran both the Venture and Viking on the Brighton road. In 1910 and 1911 only the Venture was used, and in the autumn of 1911 it was put on the Oxford to London road. Vanderbilt returned to the Brighton road from 1912–14 in which year the military authorities placed a notice on the hind boot of the coach stating that the horses were to be commandeered for army use.

Vanderbilt returned to America to review the situation and lay plans for the following year. The lure of England was too great to resist and he took passage on the last fateful voyage of the *Lusitania*. Few sportsmen were missed more than he, and a memorial was set up by his friends at Capel on the road between Dorking and Horsham over which he so frequently travelled.

John M Seabrook, the first American to be elected to the Coaching Club since Vanderbilt, driving his team of greys to the Nimrod (a drawing by Rosalind Goody).

A most unusual road

When the tide had ebbed

In 1820 two turnpike roads were opened on the route round Morecambe Bay, but they did little to attract the coaches which still went the direct way—across the sands for some ten miles between Lancaster and Ulverston. This is even more amazing as the "road" was covered by the tides of the bay for more than half the time in every day. This is reflected in the contemporary advertisements which stated that the coaches to and from Ulverston made the crossing "as tides permit".

The specially lightened coaches started from either the Kings Arms or the Commercial Inn, Lancaster, and went by way of Bridge Street which was steep and twisting, testing the coachman and his team to the fullest when they were fresh and anxious to get on with their work. From here they passed over the old Lune bridge, since demolished, and thence on for three miles from Skerton to Hest Bank on land before setting out across the sands of Morecambe Bay.

When the sands were wet and clinging it was agony for the horses who had to labour terribly to haul the often heavily laden coaches, especially as the sands were often made more treacherous by small rivulets. The time for each crossing was dictated by the tides and was usually when the tide had been on the ebb for about four hours. It was considered dangerous to cross if the tide had been coming in for more than two hours. This inevitably meant that the daily coach from Ulverston travelled the last mile or so when it was dusk so a powerful light was lit in an upper room at the Hest Bank Hotel as a beacon.

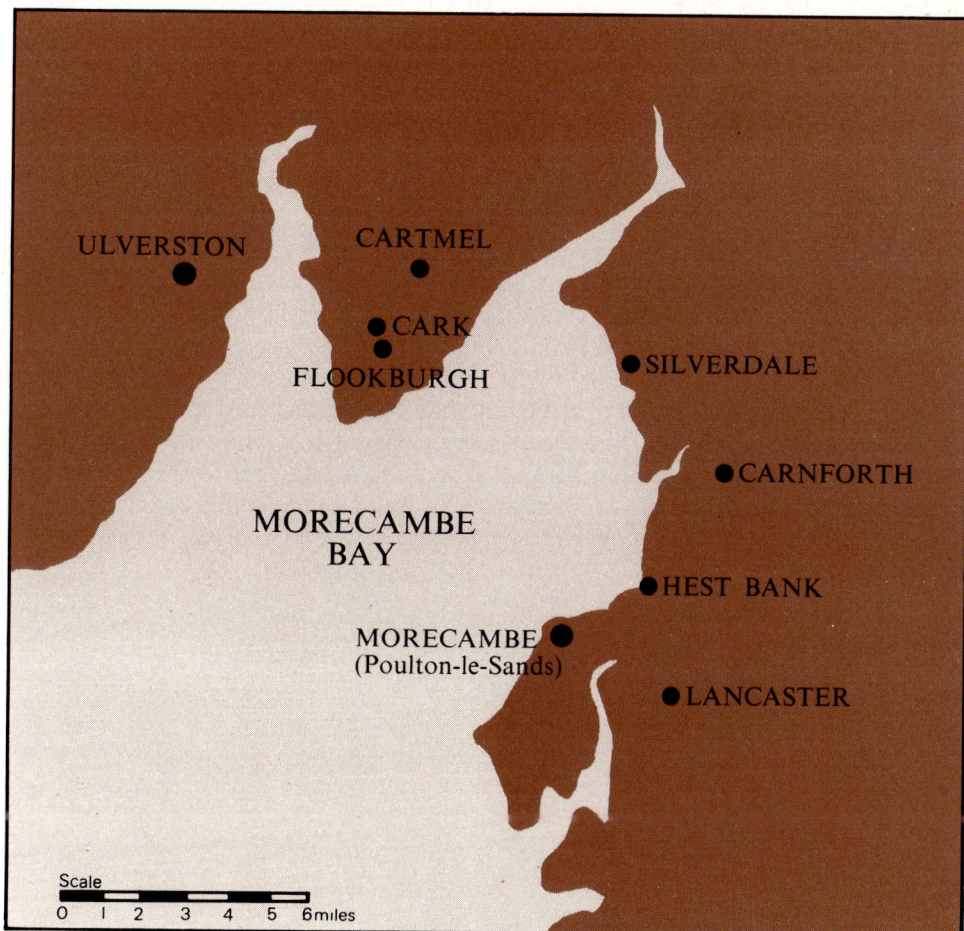

Map of Morecambe Bay showing ULVERSTON, CARTMEL, CARK, FLOOKBURGH, SILVERDALE, CARNFORTH, HEST BANK, MORECAMBE (Poulton-le-Sands) and LANCASTER. Scale 0 1 2 3 4 5 6 miles.

The most hazardous part of the journey was the crossing of the Keer, a stream of some consequence. Until 1820 each driver had his own favourite crossing place but it was now obligatory to take a mounted guide in front of the coach who carried a long pole to search out shifting sands. From here onwards for the next four miles it was good going and the coach rolled on easily on the hard sands. When they reached more streams intersecting the bay, they were met by another guide on horseback. This man was enough to frighten any passenger with his wild appearance and dirty sheepskin thrown over his horse's loins. He marked the best crossings with broom markers and when he had seen the travellers safely across he would ride up to the coach so that the passengers could show their appreciation.

It is recorded that in August 1825 a coach crossing one of the Keer channels was blown over in a gale. Happily all the passengers were saved but one of the unfortunate horses was drowned. Later the same year in another accident the coach sank to its axles in shifting sand, again without loss of life. Empty barrels were lashed to the coach for buoyancy and it was found some days later washed up on shore at Poulton-le-Sands.

In 1828 the oversands coach from Lancaster to Ulverston sank quickly in treacherous soft sand. Again everyone escaped but one nearly lost his life. He was a travelling entertainer who had been performing at Lancaster during the assizes. Anxious to save his belongings he struggled back to the coach only to be overtaken by the quicksand. Luckily he was rescued by the other passengers making a human chain.

The final part of the crossing to the shore at Cart Lane was straightforward and usually took about half an hour. The guide's cottage was a good land mark for the coachmen making their "landfall". From there the coaches proceeded on the Cartmel promontory through Flookburgh and Cark.

From this point onwards it was a relatively short journey to Ulverston, but the channel of the Leven on the far shore was deep if an error of direction was made. Another guide was on hand who would use the same method as his colleague to indicate the safe crossing with broom branches or brogs as they were known locally. His services were paid for by the Duchy of Lancaster, and the monks of Chapel Island just west of the coach route said prayers daily for the safe delivery of travellers on the sands. This coach service lasted into the railway era and there is an account of a coach being lost in 1850 on its journey between Hest Bank and Silverdale. This was perhaps the most remarkable coach road in Britain with no turnpike gate, just the wind and the tide to take toll of the unwary traveller.

Four-horse driving clubs

Oliver Cromwell was one of the first of a long line of amateur coachmen who took up driving for pleasure after he had been presented with some fine horses by the Count of Oldenburg. Perhaps he felt he could control the animals by the same methods he had used when he had taken the reins of political power in England.

Infuriated by his own ineptness at handling his high-spirited team, he set about one of the horses with a whip. Immediately the team bolted and he was thrown from the box seat. Not only did the fall cause the pistol he carried in his pocket to go off, but he was also dragged along by his foot which was caught in the harness.

Little was written about those who drove for pleasure until 1807 when it is recorded that the Bensington Driving Club was formed by twenty-five enthusiastic amateurs.

In 1808 Mr Charles Buxton and friends founded the Four Horse Club which had scarcely got on its feet before a charge of furious driving was brought against some of its youthful members who, no doubt thinking they were Roman charioteers, "received permission to resign."

The Four Horse Club lasted until 1824, but the Bensington Driving Club survived until the early eighteen-fifties. Lord Chesterfield founded the Richmond Driving Club in 1838 and with characteristic directness insisted on the members "driving like coachmen but looking like gentlemen". The club was not destined to be a success and lasted only some six seasons before its demise.

Lieutenant Colonel Trevor C Morris driving the Household Cavalry team to Ascot, 1970.
Courtesy of Mr R A Brown

HRH Prince Philip arriving at the Coaching Club centenary dinner in 1971 on the box seat of Saunders Watney's coach.

Driving for pleasure was stopped by the Crimean War, and it was not until peace was declared in 1856 that the Four-in-Hand Club was formed by thirteen founder members meeting at the home of the Marquis of Stafford.

The most significant event of the age was the founding of the Coaching Club in 1871 to cater for the overflow from the super-exclusive Four-in-Hand Club. Its founder was Lieutenant Colonel Henry Armytage who had shown his earlier enthusiasm by driving the last stage of the Weymouth stage coach at the age of seventeen.

The first meet was on June 17 1871 when twenty-two coaches were seen off on their drive from Marble Arch to Greenwich by HRH The Prince of Wales. The president, the Duke of Beaufort, wore cornflowers in his buttonhole and started a tradition which has lasted to this day. Perhaps coachmen and guards had used the cornflower as their emblem long before, but blue was the family colour of the Beauforts.

A special enclosure was put at Coaching Club members' disposal at Ascot for the races, and space was allotted at Lords for the Eton and Harrow match and the Oxford and Cambridge match from 1872 to 1914. In 1874 it was decided to cater for regimental coaches and the first to be admitted was that of the 5th Lancers in 1875. Sadly the only regimental coach now on the road belongs to the Household Cavalry.

In 1971 the 176th meet of the club celebrated the centenary, a splendid occasion followed by the fifty-first members' dinner in the Great Hall of Hampton Court Palace. HRH Prince Philip was the principal guest, and he was elected a full member in 1974.

The Duke wore cornflowers

Brakes

Down hazardous hills

The skid-pan was hung on the near side of the coach, and it was placed under the near-side rear wheel which effectively locked it, allowing the coach to descend a hill in crab fashion but under control. It was the guard's responsibility to put on and remove the skid. This operation in itself was hazardous and great care had to be exercised, especially at the bottom of the hill as the skid would be extremely hot with the friction generated by its downhill slide.

Many disasters were recorded as a result of provincial stage coaches travelling with no guard for reasons of economy, and thereby tempting the coachman to descend steep hills without stopping to get down and place the skid in its proper place under the rear wheel. In the illustration it will be seen that the skid had extended sides to stop it from becoming dislodged from the wheel. The chain is attached to a ring on the end of the skid which is exactly the right length to ensure it stays in place. It only took a few descents for the metal to wear and it was against accepted practice to bolt a new piece or iron on the base as bolt heads would wear through and possibly cause an accident.

Lord Algernon St Maur, writing in the Beaufort Library, was quick to point out that the drag shoe was far too frequently used by inexperienced coachmen. He tells us that the place to see its use in London was the top of St James's Street where the inept would make its descent look like the perilous drive down the infamous Henley Hill with a coach packed with passengers and piled with luggage. With a certain smugness he relates how he and his companions trotted down the same street with a full load, relying on his well schooled wheelers ability to hold back the coach without help.

The main disadvantage of the drag shoe was that once it was on it could not be removed until the bottom of the hill had been reached. This meant that on hills that were steep off the brow and then sloped more gently, it could not be removed after the first perilous part of the descent, and the remainder of the hill could not be trotted down at a good speed under complete control which would have been made possible by the application of the hand or pressure brake on to the steel tyres of the rear wheels.

Skid attached to its chain on the Quicksilver.

The brake blocks were originally made of chestnut which was hard enough to withstand hard wear and soft enough not to squeak unbearably as oak would. In the latter part of the coaching revival, solid rubber blocks were developed and sold in quantity. The brakes were sympathetically designed and did little to detract from the clean lines of the coaches to which they were almost universally fitted.

Even these brakes, however, were not really effective on very steep hills and the skid shoe had to be relied on as in earlier times. The mail coaches had only this effective instrument to retard them, and on easier descents the coach would rattle along at great speed held back only by the straining wheelers.

On today's slippery road surfaces most coach horses are fitted with studs in their shoes to help them gain a secure foothold. Calkins* can be used as alternatives to studs, but their use is now mainly confined to harness horses in eastern Europe.

*Calkin: protrusions of metal turned down at the ends of the horse shoe to lift the heel off the ground.

Driving a team

Imagine driving a thirty-two-foot articulated lorry without power steering or power brakes and one has some idea of the difficulties in driving four unpredictable horses.

The first surprise for the would-be coachman is the height that he sits above the horses on the highbox seat of the coach, giving a commanding view of the horses and the road ahead.

In front of him are the horses controlled by four reins coming back to the left hand. No reassuring steering wheel here—just a long and delicate series of leather reins connected to the bits in the horses' mouths, and the coachman must take up the correct one without hesitation. The correct way of holding the reins is shown in the diagram.

Sharp turns can be executed by pointing or looping the reins. If a turn to the left is necessary, then the near lead rein is picked up some six to eight inches in front of the left hand. The loop is then formed and held securely under the thumb. The wheelers must now be prevented from following too soon and effectively cutting the corner. This is achieved by looping the off-wheel rein in opposition.

When the leaders have rounded the corner the loop governing their reins is released first, followed by the loop of the wheel rein. A turn to the right is made by taking a loop on the off lead rein and taking opposition on the near wheel rein. Slight deviations of course can be made by turning the hand and moving it across the body.

In taking up a loop, a good coachman should never lean forward. The loop must always be made by bringing it back to the left hand which must never be moved forward to accommodate the loop. It is always the sign of a novice or inept coachman if he "climbs down the reins" when driving, and a good firm position is important if an elegant style is to be cultivated.

As the wheelers are the only horses capable of stopping the coach when it is going downhill, the leaders must be out of draught on reaching the brow of a hill. If they are inadvertently allowed to go into their collars, they will probably pull the wheelers off their feet, and disaster may result.

It is also important to start the coach correctly. The initial impetus must come from the wheelers who should be leaning into their collars ready for the signal "Walk on". If the leaders attempt to start the coach there is a real danger of breaking a main bar or of the horses jibbing.

After a short while the learner will find his arm tiring, so he must hand over the reins to his experienced companion before this becomes acute. In early lessons this is often aggravated by a nervous tensing of the muscles which the coachman must learn to relax.

The whip should always be carried in the right hand and should be held at forty-five degrees across the body. It should rest happily in the hand if it is properly balanced and should never be cracked. Its main purpose is to maintain impulsion, but it must never be used to hit a horse unnecessarily or unfairly. Many stories are told of the coachman's skill with the whip including removing a

Four-in-hand
how to hold reins

Leaders

Lead bars
or single bars

Crab

Main bar

Head terret

Pole chain

Wheelers

Details of reins and bars on a team

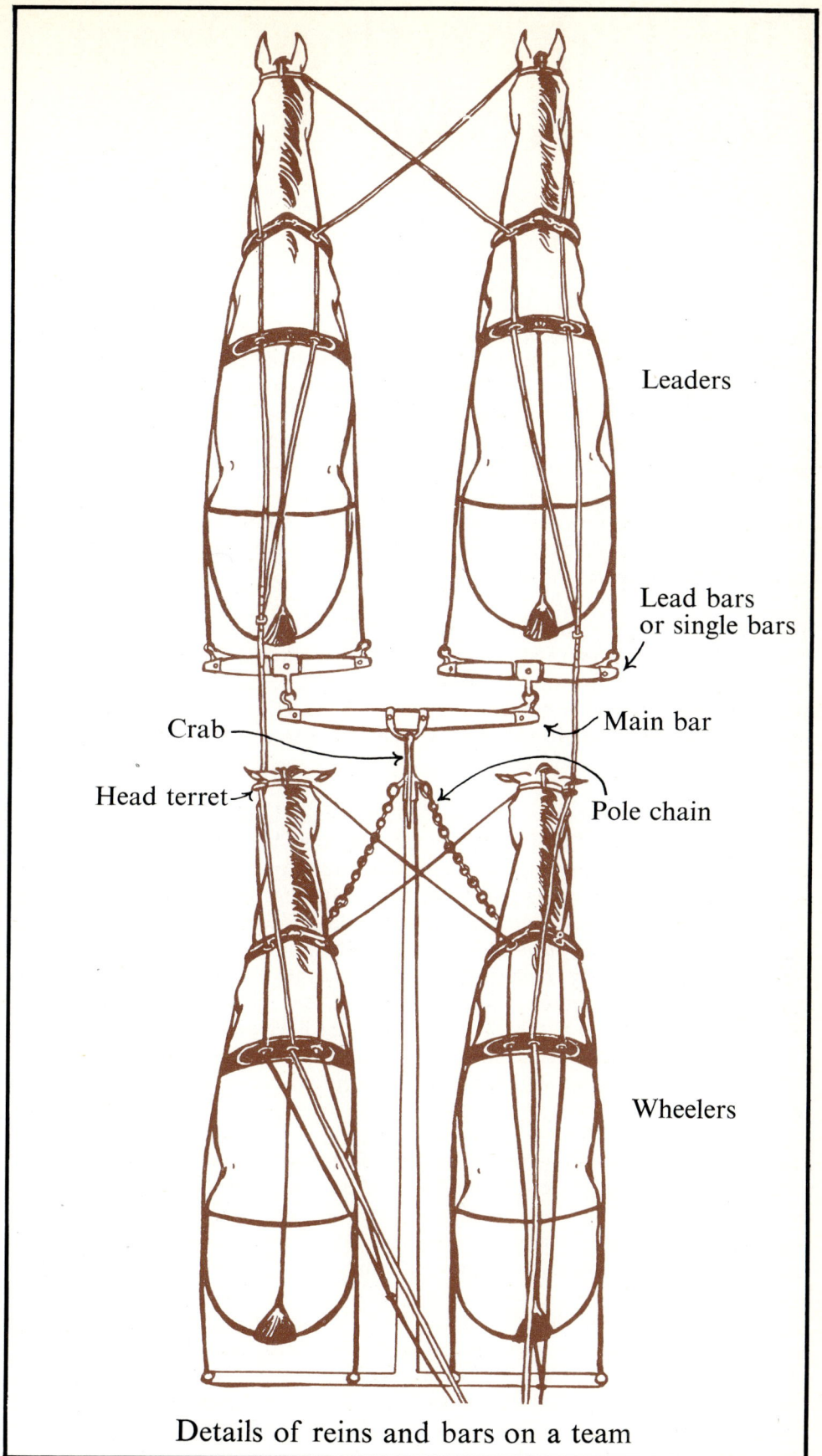

cuckoo from a nest in one deft movement and picking a fly off a leader's right eyelid with friendly dexterity.

The good coachman will see that the work is evenly shared and that each horse is doing his fair share. Above all, he must resist the temptation of continually adjusting the reins. This is bad practice as it only upsets the horses and looks most unworkmanlike.

There is no substitute for experience, and a good apprenticeship on the box must be served.

Old Lal on the Great North Road

The road between the Peacock, Islington, and the Sugar Loaf, Dunstable, was the haunt of one of the best known characters who lived on the fringe of coaching. Old Lal was born legless but was a well known sight driving his four-in-hand of foxhounds to a primitive small carriage. Such was the speed of his hounds that they would overtake the coaches so that their master could solicit tips at the end of the stage from their passengers.

The whole effect was very sporting, and Old Lal was known for his well matched hounds and their excellent turnout which would have been a credit to their equestrian counterparts.

He was well known to Tom Hennesy, the celebrated coachman of the Stamford Regent, and all who travelled on the northern coaches. It is recorded that there were twenty or more drawn up outside the Peacock at seven o'clock in the morning and included such famous names as the York Highflyer, the Leeds Union and the York Express, from which a rich harvest could be gleaned by the coachman of the foxhound team.

Old Lal always could count on a bed at the Sugar Loaf, Dunstable, or more precisely the hay loft of that establishment where he had made friends with the horsekeeper, Daniel Sleigh. It was here that the hounds found their food and their master spent long hours polishing their neat set of harness. As he travelled the road he would find shelter where he could and return "home" when his fortunes allowed. Often he would rest one of the hounds and would go out the following day with the remaining three harnessed trandem to his vehicle. Baron Faverot de Kerbrech writing in his *L'Art de Conduire et d'Atteler* describes a trandem—three abreast— as "attelage d'eveque" or "bishop's team". The lack of one hound made little difference to his speed over the ground but naturally his tips were not as large as when he was driving his extraordinary team.

Daniel Sleigh was a good companion for Old Lal as he had little time for any man except this eccentric cripple and he had become regarded as a recluse. His life was with horses and he never ventured further than the forge with a horse that wanted shoeing. It was he, however, who kept the old man's sporting clothes in good order like a well trained valet.

Little is known of how Old Lal met his death. A search for him was started when he had been missing for several days and eventually he was found near the remains of his vehicle which was stuck between the trunks of two large trees. One hound had been killed in the spill and the others had desperately chewed their way through their harness and released themselves. It was assumed that they had seen a fox near the road and had given chase with their unfortunate coachman unable to do anything about it.

The spot where the accident happened became accepted as a place to be avoided after dark. Those who lived nearby recounted tales of a legless phantom coachman driving a team of hounds in pursuit of their prey.

A four-in-hand of hounds

The Tantivy Trot

The Tantivy left London for Birmingham at 7 am. By 7 pm it had covered the 125 miles at an average speed of over eleven miles an hour, allowing one hour for changing horses and for the refreshment of the passengers. It could not, however, claim to be the fastest coach as this accolade went to the Shrewsbury Wonder and Manchester Telegraph.

The name Tantivy was derived from the imitative sound bringing to mind the sound of the huntsman's horn and giving an image of speed and dash. Cracknell was its celebrated coachman and drove between London and Oxford and once covered the whole 125 miles at one stretch. The Tantivy Trot was written in his honour by Rowland Egerton Warburton, of Arley Hall, Cheshire, in 1834, and it was sung to the tune of "Here's to the Maiden of Bashful Fifteen". The "Poet Laureate" of the coaching world captured the spirit of a departing era and foresaw accurately the coming of the railways and the fateful consequences for coach travel.

Music of the road

THE TANTIVY TROT

Here's to the heroes of four-in hand fame,
   Harrison, Peyton, and Warde, sir;
Here's to the dragsmen that after them came,
   Ford, and the Lancashire lord, sir.

Here's to the team, sir, all harnessed to start,
   Brilliant in Brummagem leather;
Here's to the waggoner skill'd in the art
   Of coupling the cattle together.

Here's to the arm that holds them when gone,
   Still to a gallop inclined, sir;
Heads to the front with no bearing reins on,
   Tails with no cruppers behind, sir.

Here's to the shape that is shown the near side,
   Here's to the blood on the off, sir;
Limbs without check to the freedom of stride,
   Wind without whistle or cough, sir.

On and off the road

A miscellania of coaching

The galloping stage. On 13 July 1888, the famous professional whip, James Selby, drove the Old Times from London to Brighton and back for a wager in the record-breaking time of seven hours and fifty minutes.

Dick Turpin's flight through Edmonton.
Radio Times Hulton Picture Library

In 1874 a Mr Ernest Hargreaves, of Tunbridge Wells, was so anxious to become a member of the Coaching Club that he resolved to drive 1 000 miles in a year. He took a team of twenty-one horses and the road coach, The Sportsman, to the Lake District, making Bowness his headquarters. Here he drove from Windermere to Keswick and back each day. His health broke down before the end of the season, and he had to give up driving, and his name was withdrawn from the candidates book.

The Hero in the stable yard at Burton Constable Hall, Hull.

I says to our Governor says I—
keep your eye on them ere Leaders George

THE GUARD WOT LOOKS ARTER THE
SOVEREIGN

Published on 20 April 1829.

The Old Berkeley coach, one of only three quarter-size coaches made by Mills of Paddington. John Richards had the pleasure of riding on the Old Berkeley at the Royal Winter Fair in Toronto in 1973 when it was owned and driven by Mrs Ailsa Crawford who enjoyed great success with her team of Welsh ponies.
Photograph by kind permission of Sotheby Parke Bernet

COACHING DINNER AT GREENWICH Copy of a letter sent by a coaching enthusiast to a friend in 1872 (the year the club was founded) who was arranging a dinner at Greenwich, after one of the first meets of the club.

The party on my coach will consist of seven men, besides myself. Eight I hold the golden number, never to be exceeded without weakening the efficiency of concentration.

The dinner is to consist of turtle, followed by no other fish than whitebait, which is to be followed by no other meat but grouse, which are to be succeeded simply by apple fritters and jelly, pastry on such occasions being quite out of place.

With the turtle of course there will be punch; with the whitebait, champagne; and with the grouse, claret. The two former I have ordered to be particularly well iced, and they will all be placed in succession upon the table, so that we can help ourselves as we please. I shall permit no other wines, unless, perchance a bottle or two of port, if particularly wanted, as I hold a variety of wines a great mistake.

With respect to the adjuncts, please take care that there is cayenne, with lemons cut into halves, not in quarters, within reach of everyone for the turtle, and that brown bread and butter in abundance is set upon the table for the whitebait.

It is no trouble to think of these little matters before hand, but they make a vast difference in convivial contentment. The dinner will be followed by ices, and a good dessert, after which coffee and one glass of liqueur each, and no more, so that the present may be enjoyed without introducing retrospective regrets.

As you know, if the master of a feast wishes his party to succeed, he must know how to command, and not let his guests run riot, each according to his own wild fancy.

by courtesy of Mr R. A. Brown

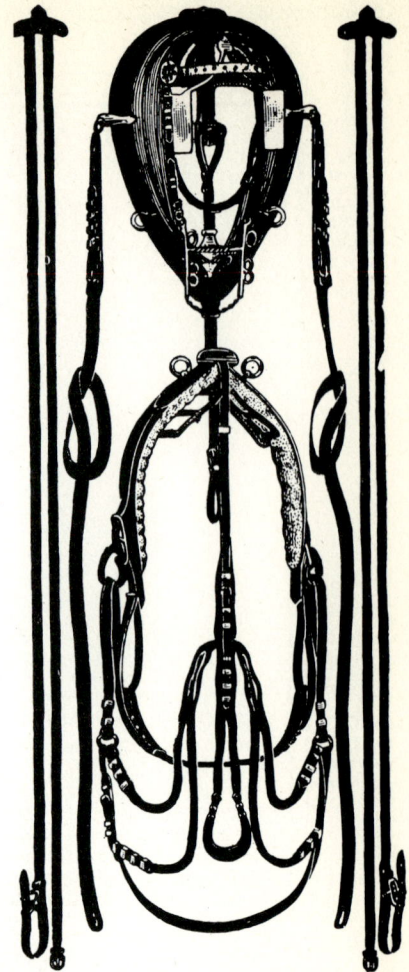

Single harness hanging on wall-mounted iron brackets.
Illustration by kind permission of Sotheby Parke Bernet

Outside the Royal Albiontic in Brighton, about 1867–68, is Mr Chandos Pole's coach and four. Mr Pole is on the box with his favourite professional, Alfred Tedder, in the box seat. The lone passenger is believed to be Mr B. J. (Cherry) Angell.
Photograph from The Carriage Journal, USA

HEDON AND PATTRINGTON TURNPIKE ROAD

Table of Tolls to be taken at the Haven Side

Horses or Beasts, Drawing any Coach, Chariot, Landau, Berlin, Chaise, Hearse, ~~...~~

If 6 Horses or Beasts _ _ _	2½ each
If 4 or 5 Horses or Beasts _ _ _	3 each
If 2 Horses or Beasts _ _ _	4½ each
If 1 Horse or Beast _ _ _ _ _	4½

Horses or Beasts, Drawing any Waggon, Wain, Cart, Dray, or any Carriage with fellies of Six Inches,

If 3 or more Horses or Beasts	2½ each
If 2 Horses or Beasts _ _ _ _	3 each
If 1 Horse or Beast _ _ _ _ _	4

Horses or Beasts Drawing any Waggon, Wain, Cart, Dray or any such Carriage with fellies of four and an half Inches and not Six Inches,

If 3 or more Horses or Beasts	3 each
If 2 Horses or Beasts _ _ _ _	4 each
If 1 Horse or Beast _ _ _ _	5

Horses or Beasts, Drawing any Waggon, Wain, Cart, Dray or any such Carriage with fellies of less than four and an half Inches,

If 3 or more Horses or Beasts	3½ each
If 2 Horses or Beasts _ _ _ _	4½ each
If 1 Horse or Beast _ _ _ _	6

Every Horse or Beast drawing any Carriage not before described _	4½
Every Horse or Beast laden or unladen and not drawing _ _ _ _	1½
A score of Oxen or neat Cattle _ _ _ _	10)
A score of Calves, Sheep, Lambs or Swine	5) And so in proportion for a less number

Cattle drawing stage Coaches, stage Waggons, Vans, Caravans or other stage Carriages carrying passengers or goods for payment, hire or reward, having paid Toll, and returning the same day to pay again on repassing the Bar, and Horses drawing post Chaises and other Carriages travelling for hire to pay every time passing with a fresh hiring

Wm WATSON,
Clerk to the Trustees of the said Turnpike

Hedon, July 1852

List of tolls payable on the Hedon to Patrington turnpike road, East Yorkshire. A wooden gauge was used to measure the width of the fellies (the wooden rims of the wheels). The wider the wheel, the lower the toll, as this would cause least damage to the soft road surface. Kingston-upon-Hull City Museums

The York coach—a mishap.

Victor Venner.

The Bath coach at the Half-Way House.

The Light of other Days

Out of his Element

NARCISSUS & Cº

SNOBKINS

Ce cher Jules!

BARON SHENTPERSHENT

The Heiress & Her Cousin

THE COUNTESS

MOTHER AND DAUGHTER

Not yet Out of the World

4 in Hand

DOUBTFUL

TINY of the 4th LIFE GUARDS

IN THE DRIVE

THE MYSTERIOUS STRANGER

No Doubt!

H. Harral Sc

*Wood engraving by Horace Harral from a London newspaper
published between 1860 and 1870.*

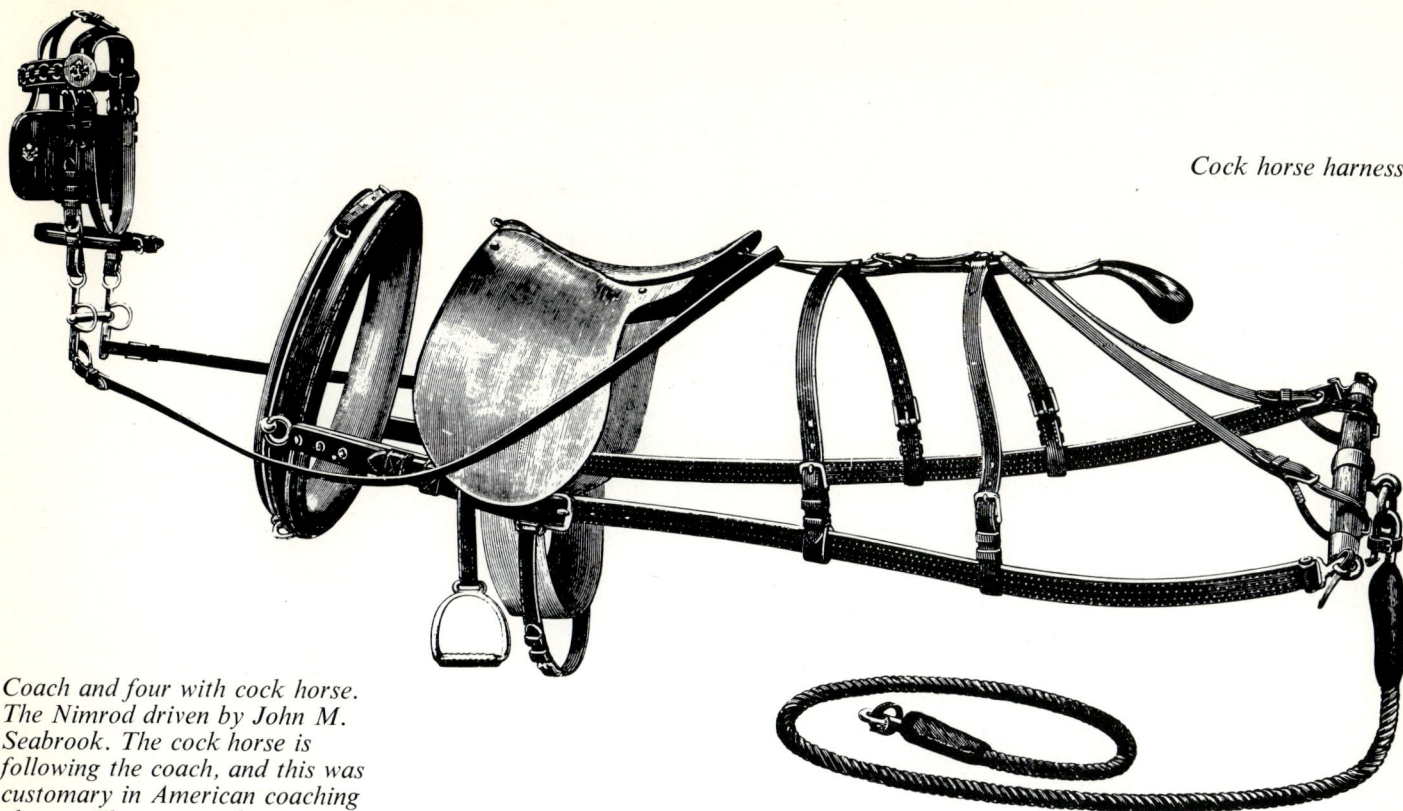

Cock horse harness.

Coach and four with cock horse. The Nimrod driven by John M. Seabrook. The cock horse is following the coach, and this was customary in American coaching classes. The practice has now lapsed.

ROYAL HOTEL COACH OFFICE, Cheltenham.

IMPROVED SAFETY & ELEGANT LIGHT POST COACHES,
DAILY TO THE FOLLOWING PLACES.

LONDON The Magnet Safety Coach, every Morning at ½ past Six o'clock thro' Northleach, Burford, Witney, Oxford, Henley, Maidenhead, Slough & Hounslow.

LONDON Royal Veteran, every Morning at ½ past Eight thro' Northleach, Burford, Witney, Oxford, Wycomb & Uxbridge.

OXFORD & LONDON Two Day Coach, every day except Sundays at Twelve o'clock. Sleeps at Oxford.

OXFORD Coaches, every Morning at ½ past Six & ½ past Eight o'clock.

BATH The Original Post Coach, every day except Sundays at Nine o'clock through Gloucester & Rodborough.

BATH The York House Coach, every day except Sundays at Two o'clock through Painswick & Stroud.

BRISTOL The Traveller, every day except Sundays at Twelve o'clock thro' Gloucester & Newport.

BRISTOL The Royal Pilot, through Gloucester every Monday, Wednesday, & Friday, at ½ past One o'clock.

EXETER The Traveller, every day except Sundays, at Twelve thro' Gloucester, Bristol, Bridgewater, Taunton, Wellington, Collumpton, & Exeter, where it meets Coaches for Plymouth.

GLOUCESTER Accommodation Coaches every Morning at Nine, ½ past Nine & Twelve, o'clock, Afternoon at ½ past One, Three, Five & Seven o'clock, in the Evening.

TEWKESBURY Coaches every Morning except Sundays, at Eight & Twelve, Afternoon at ½ past One, every Evening at 8.

MALVERN The Mercury, every Morning at ½ before Eight, except Sundays, to Essington's Hotel, Malvern Wells, arrives at Eleven o'clock, leaves Malvern at Five.

LIVERPOOL The Magnet, every Tuesday, Thursday & Saturday, at Twelve o'clock, thro' Worcester, Birmingham, Walsall, Stafford, Stone, & Newcastle.

LIVERPOOL The Aurora, every day except Sundays, at ½ past one o'clock sleeping at Birmingham.

MANCHESTER The Traveller, every day except Sundays, at Twelve o'clock, thro' Worcester, Sleeping at Birmingham.

SHEFFIELD The Amity, every day except Sundays, at Twelve o'clock, through Burton, Derby, & Chesterfield.

CHESTER The Dispatch, every day except Sundays, thro' Newport & Fernhill.

BIRMINGHAM The Traveller, thro' Worcester, every day except Sundays, at Twelve o'clock.

BIRMINGHAM The York House Coach thro' Worcester every day except Sundays, at ½ past One o'clock.

BIRMINGHAM The Mercury, thro' Worcester, every Morning at Eight.

WORCESTER Coaches, every Morning at Eight & Twelve, also at ½ past one o'clock, in the Afternoon.

WOLVERHAMPTON The Everlasting, every Morning at Eight, except Sundays.

COVENTRY The Pilot, thro' Evesham, Alcester, Stratford, Warwick, & Leamington, every day except Sundays, at ½ past one o'clock.

FLY WAGGONS & VANS TO LONDON
on Tuesdays Thursdays & Saturdays at Twelve o'clock & arrives the following Night

THOMAS HAINES Junr. & Co. ——— PROPRIETORS.

NB. Every possible comfort & accommodation afforded to those who may be pleased to honour this Establishment with their patronage.

COACHES SENT TO ANY PART OF THE TOWN TO TAKE UP IF REQUIRED.

This was the dress for the well turned-out amateur whip at the turn of the century. The coat would invariably be box cloth or Melton cloth. The checked trousers were known as sponge-bag.

Mail Coach

WE'RE LOSING FAST THE GOOD, OLD DAYS
OF RATTLING WHEELS
AND GALLANT GREYS;
WE'RE LOSING FAST THE LUGGAGED ROOF,
THE WHISTLING GUARD
AND RINGING HOOF;

THE ENGLISH STAGE
AND HIGH—BRED TEAMS
WILL SOON EXIST BUT IN OUR DREAMS;
AND WHIRLING MAIL
OR STARTLING HORN
NE'ER CHEER THE NIGHT,
NOR ROUSE THE MORN.
AH, WELL-A-DAY! NO CRACKING LASH,
NO CHAMPING BIT, NO RESTLESS DASH,
NO "PULL UP" AT THE
"CROSS" OR "CROWN"
'MID ALL THE GOSSIPS OF THE TOWN;
FOR TIME, WITH DEEP
RAILROADED BROW,
CHANGES ALL THINGS
BUT·HORSES, NOW.
ELIZA COOK.

Four-in-harness.

The leaders of the Red Rover. It was customary to put the appropriate initials—or device—of the coach on the harness.

Turnpike
ROAD,

FROM CONGLETON TO COLLEY BRIDGE,
AND FROM
The said Bridge to SMITHY GREEN,
In the Parish of Prestbury, in the County of Chester.

Notice is hereby given,

That the **TOLLS** to arise at the several Toll-gates erected upon the said Road, **WILL BE PUT UP**

To be LET by AUCTION,

TO THE BEST BIDDER OR BIDDERS,

At the house of Mr. JOHN HODKINSON, the Old Angel Inn, in Macclesfield,

In the County of Chester,

On TUESDAY the 29th JULY NEXT,

Precisely at One o'Clock in the Afternoon,

In the manner directed by the Acts of Parliament passed in the Third and Fourth Years of the Reign of his present Majesty King George the Fourth, for regulating Turnpike Roads, for the Term of One Year, to commence on the *Tenth Day of September next*, at Twelve o'Clock at Noon, subject to such conditions as will be then produced, and which Gates are let the present Year at the several Sums set opposite thereto, clear of all Deductions, viz.

Dane Bower Bank Gate & Chain, and Hallgreave Gate & Chains, £180
Colley Lane Gate and Harding's Bank Gate and Chains, - - - 162

The Gates will be put up at those Sums, and whoever happen to be the Takers, must at the same time, give security with sufficient Sureties to the Satisfaction of the Trustees then present, for payment of the Rent or Rents agreed for in such manner as they shall direct.

JOHN CRUSO,

Clerk to the Trustees of the said Road.

LEEK, 24TH JUNE, 1828.

Bayley, Printer, Macclesfield.

The revenues from the Congleton turnpike road are put up for auction. The original document is in the archives at Gawsworth Hall, Cheshire.

The masterful mind

The question may be asked: why do you want to risk losing your composure, annoying your bank manager and consulting your doctor so as to put together a team of horses for coaching? The answer is straightforward: it's a challenge to a man who loves horses. There has probably never been the perfect team on the road and there is always one horse out of the four that in some little way fails to achieve the standard set in the mind of the coachman.

When putting young horses in harness for the first time there is the thrill of anticipation that the splendid animal first spied out hunting or in the dealer's yard will fulfil all one's hopes—often dashed when the recruit is unhappy in his new environment and is not keen to spend the next few years of his life pulling a coach along the leafy lanes and the city streets of Britain.

It may also be said that the team tends to adopt the outlook on life that emanates from their master, rather in accordance with the old adage that people tend to look like their dogs. In the same way, the team will adopt the characteristics, good or bad, of their coachman.

Days of rain, chill winds and quizzical looks from baffled onlookers may have to be endured for the one day when everything goes near perfectly with the horses and coachmen in tune—a time to be looked back on and savoured. Horses, like humans, have their off days, and the coachman must be prepared to recognise this and help soothe the temper of a leader upset by his partner not doing his share of the work.

Most horse lore is sheer common sense, but there is no doubt that the horse instinctively knows if he is being driven by a masterful, decisive coachman.

The Dalmatian has a natural affinity with horses and can easily be trained to run under the carriage, originally to guard the contents but he is now often seen as part of the elegant equipage.

When the guard has resumed his seat and John Richards has given the command "Walk on", the patient Dalmatian will take up his position under the coach.

No man living could hold a team of horses if they should determine to set away, and it is only by deceiving them that he can exercise full control by using his superior intellect.

On those rare occasions when the horses take matters into their own hands and bolt, the first and most sensible thing for the coachman to do is to point them immediately at a thick hedge which will stop them effectively with the minimum of damage to all concerned. The old coachman, in conditions far different from those of today, seeing the road clear ahead for some considerable distance, would spur his team on at great speed and put the brake on as hard as possible. This would soon tire the horses, especially if the road was uphill, and then he would make them go on long after they wanted to stop. When he eventually decided to pull up it would be he who gave the word and his will would have prevailed. Naturally this plan would be suicide on today's crowded roads.

The horse handled in the right way has so much to give to a sympathetic master and is a generous and good friend. His lot now is much improved on that of his forebears. He is an anachronism, but he has survived because the horseman is inseparable from his horse.

95

"Walk on"

When man had succeeded in domesticating the horse he put it to all manner of uses in his service. Its noblest calling was perhaps on the roads of Britain in the Golden Age of Coaching which was to span so short a time. This period is well documented by contemporary artists and writers who put on record the scenes of an epoch in Britain's history which was a paradise for the sportsman.

The pages of this book are filled with larger-than-life characters who had a complete knowledge of the exacting skills of horsemanship which were necessary if the teams of high-mettled horses were to keep to their demanding schedules. Most of the coachmen had risen from the ranks of the ostlers and in general they were not sufficiently literate to put pen to paper so the niceties of the art were transmitted by word of mouth and observation.

The coaching revival was inspired by amateur coachmen who had travelled to their public schools by stagecoach and wished to recreate the excitement and adventure they remembered so well in their youth. Men such as Corbett, Lennox and Reynardson were able to set down their reminiscences which ensured that the true stories of the coach roads of England were not forgotten. Many of these appeared around the turn of the century, a time that was to prove such a landmark in the history of transport. The advent of the motor car was to have a profound effect and life was never to be the same again.

Commodore Chauncey Stillman's words mirror the feeling of a young American faced with a changing world:

> *No child of today, even in the country, can know the quietness of those drowsy summer afternoons when the sun seemed to stand still in an unsmirched sky, and the only sounds were the locusts' rasping song and the whirr of the lawn-mower drawn by a leather-booted old horse. The counterpart in rural England is idyllically depicted in Siegfried Sassoon's 'Memoirs of a Fox-Hunting Man'. It all seemed fixed for ever, but . . . signs of change were creeping on us.*

In the less palmy days of the 1970s interest in coaching is undiminished. Major agricultural shows hold coaching marathons which continue to attract a large entry and provide an unparalleled spectacle for anyone even remotely interested in the horse.

The story of coaching is not yet told and who knows what the future has in store for generations of coachmen as yet unborn? I am optimistic as we are all becoming more interested and concerned about our heritage and I am certain that future generations will still believe, as I do, that to sit behind four high-couraged horses is the greatest privilege given to man in his efforts to have

Dominion over . . . every living thing that moveth.